NICCOLÒ MACHIAVELLI was born in Florence in 1469. In 1498 he received an appointment to the chancellery of the Florentine Republic, serving as both an administrator and a diplomat. Machiavelli traveled to France and to Germany and knew political leaders throughout Italy, most significantly, Cesare Borgia, presumably the model for *The Prince*.

Machiavelli's official political life ended fifteen years later with the return to power of the Medici. Following his dismissal and banishment, he was accused of complicity, imprisoned, and tortured. Although exonerated, he was without position and retired to his meager farm near San Casciano. It was in this bucolic setting of near poverty and of days passed in prosaic discourse with the local peasantry that Machiavelli wrote *The Prince* and *The Discourses*, determined to prove that banishment had made him neither idle nor ineffective. He addressed *The Prince* to Lorenzo de'Medici, fervently desiring to induce the prince to emulate his creation—the ruler who would return Florence to its former glory. The city-states of Renaissance Italy had fallen into a morass of inept rulers and foreign domination; it was a time for desperate measures.

Machiavelli died in 1527. For centuries his reputation held that he had been inspired by the devil. But the man who gave his name to duplicity was in his own time a lover of liberty, a loyal patriot and a well-intentioned citizen working in behalf of his beloved Florence.

THE PRINCE

NICCOLÒ MACHIAVELLI

With selections from THE DISCOURSES

Translated by Daniel Donno

Edited and with an Introduction
by Daniel Donno

BANTAM CLASSIC

THE PRINCE AND SELECTED DISCOURSES
A Bantam Book

PUBLISHING HISTORY
The Prince was first published in 1513
First Bantam publication / October 1966
Bantam Classic edition / March 1981
Bantam Classic reissue / January 2003

Published by
Bantam Dell
A Division of Random House, Inc.
New York, New York

Library of Congress Catalog Card Number: 66-25554

ISBN 0-553-21278-8

OPM   43   42

CONTENTS

Discourses Upon the First Ten Books of Titus Livy

BOOK ONE

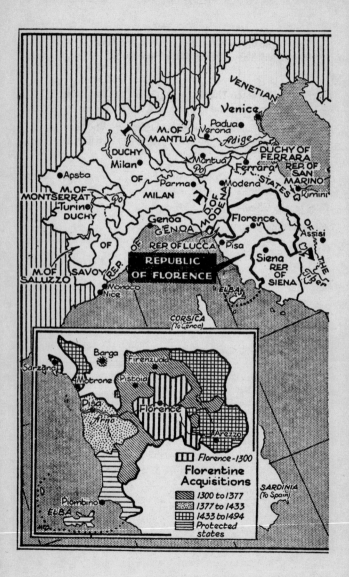

VENETIAN

Venice

Padua
Verona

Adige

M. OF
MANTUA

DUCHY
Milan

OF

MILAN

Montua

Po

DUCHY OF
FERRARA

Ferrara

REP. OF
SAN
MARINO

Rimini

Apsta

M. OF
MONTSERRAT

Turin

DUCHY

Parma

Modena

Genoa
GENOA

OF REP. OF LUCCA

Pisa

Florence

STATES

OF

Assisi

THE

OF

SAVOY

REP.

M. OF
SALUZZO

Monaco
Nice

REPUBLIC
OF FLORENCE

ELBA

Siena
REP.
OF
SIENA

the Tiber

CORSICA
(To Genoa)

Sarzana

Barga

Firenzuola

Metrone

Pistoia

Pisa

Arno

Florence

Arezzo

Piombino

ELBA

||| Florence - 1300

**Florentine
Acquisitions**

1300 to 1377

1377 to 1433

1433 to 1494

Protected
states

SARDINIA
(To Spain)

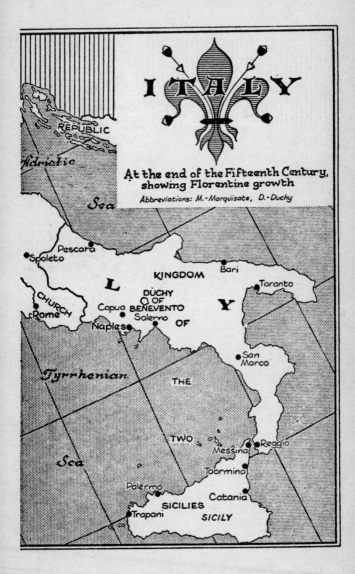

ITALY

At the end of the Fifteenth Century,
showing Florentine growth

Abbreviations: M.-Marquisate, D.-Duchy

REPUBLIC

Adriatic

Sea

Spoleto
Pescara

KINGDOM
Bari

L

CHURCH
Rome

DUCHY
OF
BENEVENTO

Capua

Salerno

Naples

OF

Taranto

Y

San
Marco

Tyrrhenian

THE

TWO

Messina
Reggio

Taormina

Sea

Palermo

Catania

SICILIES

SICILY

Trapani

INTRODUCTION

I T IS a commonplace irony that *The Prince*—the classic handbook on power politics—should have owed its birth to the collapse of its author's own political career and to the practical failure of his most cherished military innovation.

Machiavelli's official entry into politics occurred in 1498 with his appointment as Secretary to the Second Chancery of the Signoria, a position rather loosely defined, involving him in military matters as well as domestic and foreign affairs. In this post he remained until the fall of the Florentine Republic in 1512. Through all his years in office, despite pronounced reservations about the generally conciliatory policies of his government, he remained loyal to it and served his superiors with tireless energy. When Pier Soderini was elected Gonfalonier, or chief magistrate, of the Republic in 1502, Machiavelli became one of his most trusted assistants. He was assigned to important missions both in Italy and abroad. The lengthy reports he submitted in the performance of these duties bear evidence of his sagacity as an observer, quick and sure in locating the center of power in any political situation and accurate in assessing its strength, but somewhat unskilled in the game of man-to-man diplomacy. They also attest to his passionate concern for the security of his homeland and his readiness to seek solutions that lay beyond the strict limits of his professional competence and authority. He was also ordered to draw up proposals on some of the vexing issues facing the Republic. These reveal in capsule form some of the important ideas we find in his later political writings.

Perhaps his finest hour came in 1509 when, after a fifteen-year struggle, the Florentines finally reduced Pisa into submission. Much of the credit for this feat belongs to Machiavelli. Though by no means a military man, he actually directed the land and sea blockade that brought about Pisa's capitulation. Moreover, the civilian troops who had manned the operation had come into being at his insistence and had been trained under his supervision. On this occasion his conviction, one which runs like a refrain through nearly all of his political writings—that a healthy state must rely solely upon its own citizen forces in war—bore fruit. It was to do otherwise three years later at Prato, when Machiavelli's career and the Republic foundered together.

Perhaps the real cause of this calamitous event goes back to Soderini's insistence upon friendship with France as a cardinal rule of his foreign policy. Costly and difficult as it often proved, this policy nevertheless served to protect Florence from the threats of her powerful neighbors so long as France continued to count in the affairs of the peninsula. In 1511, however, Pope Julius II (together with Venice, Spain, and England) organized the Holy League and launched a campaign to drive the French out of Italy. During the war that ensued both the Holy League and the French sought assistance from Florence, but Soderini, having sent a token force to the French, tried to avoid serious entanglement. The result was that Florence incurred the enmity of both parties and (as Machiavelli could have predicted) faced the likelihood of being pounced upon by whichever side emerged the winner. To avoid this danger, Soderini then labored to arm the Republic, relying not upon mercenaries, as had so often been done before, but upon a citizen militia of the sort that had proved its merit—so it seemed—in the struggle with Pisa. Machiavelli, the prime mover of this innovation, had doubtless inspired Soderini with some of his own confidence in it. Thus when the Holy League—thanks to the last-minute intervention of the Swiss—triumphed over the French, the scene of action shifted quickly to the frontiers of the Republic. Spanish troops, accompanied by Cardinal de' Medici, soon appeared and demanded the overthrow of the government. Assured that the unfledged forces Machiavelli had recruited could withstand the invader, Soderini refused to give way. The Spaniards then attacked, choosing Prato—heavily garrisoned with green recruits—as their target. After only a short struggle the enemy effected a breach in the city wall, poured through, overwhelmed the fleeing defenders, and sacked the town completely.

This was on August 29, 1512. Two days later Soderini resigned and went into exile. The Medici, after an absence of eighteen years, reassumed control of Florence. Six weeks after Prato, Machiavelli was dismissed from office and banished from the city for the term of one year. Thus the scene was set for *The Prince* and *The Discourses*.

But not quite. Early in 1513 Machiavelli was suspected of complicity in a plot to overthrow the Medici government. He was arrested, tortured, and soon after released, his innocence having been satisfactorily established. The incident should have destroyed any lingering hope of a rapid reentry into politics under the new rulers, but *The Prince* itself is ample evidence that it had no such effect.

Machiavelli withdrew to the meager farm near San Casciano which his father had left him. There impending poverty troubled him, though he had been short of funds before. But enforced idleness in rustic surroundings for this restless man of forty-three was an entirely new burden. Throughout his fourteen years of service he had been a high-level functionary. He had visited some of the key trouble spots of his day and had represented the Republic on difficult missions in France, in Germany, in Rome, and in the petty courts of Italian princelings. He had dealt with some of the leading figures of his age, the movers and shakers of his world. Now, in Polonius' words, he was reduced to

> be no assistant for a state
> But keep a farm and carters.

How he reacted to this suddenly slackened tempo and reduced circumstances we know from a letter he wrote to his friend Francesco Vettori less than a year later. The mingling of trifling details with serious matters, the shifting of tone, alternating between genial humor and hints of despair, are typical of Machiavelli's familiar letters in which the salient features of his mind and character stand out strikingly:

. . . What my life is, I will tell you. I get up at sunrise and go to a grove of mine which I am having chopped down. I spend a couple of hours there, checking up on the work of the previous day and passing the time with the woodcutters, who are never without some trouble or other, either among themselves or with the neighbors. On the subject of this grove, I could tell you a host of interesting things that have happened involving Frosino da Panzano and others who wanted some of the wood. Frosino in particular sent for a few cords of it without telling me, and when it came to paying he wanted to hold back ten lire because he claimed I owed him that much as winnings from a game of *cricca* we played four years ago at the home of Antonio Guicciardini. I began to raise the devil. I wanted to accuse the carter who had come for it of theft. But Giovanni Machiavelli came between us and made us settle. Battista Guicciardini, Filippo Ginori, Tommaso del Bene, and certain other citizens each ordered a cord when that ill wind was blowing.* I promised some to all of them and sent a cord to Tommaso. But it turned out to be only half a cord after it reached Florence because he, his wife, his servants, and children were all there helping to stack it. . . . Finally, seeing who was making the profit on it, I told the others that I had no more wood, whereupon they all made quite a fuss—especially Battista, who ranks this with the other misfortunes of Prato.**

When I leave the grove, I go to a spring and from there to my bird snares. I carry a book under my arm—Dante or Petrarch, or one of the minor poets like Tibullus, Ovid, or the like. I read about their amorous passions, and their loves call my own to mind, so I delight a while in these thoughts. Then I betake myself to the inn on the highway. I chat with the people going by, ask for news from their home towns, learn a few things, and note the various tastes and curious notions of men. Meanwhile lunchtime arrives and, together with my family, I eat whatever food my poor house and scanty patrimony afford. Having lunched, I return to the inn. There I generally find the innkeeper, a butcher, a miller, and two kiln-tenders. In their company I idle the rest of the day away playing at *cricca* and *tricchetrach*—games that give rise to a host of quarrels, cutting remarks, and insults. Often we fight over a

---

*That is, when Machiavelli was arrested.
**Battista Guicciardini was Governor of Prato when it was sacked.

penny and are heard yelling as far off as San Casciano. Set down among these lice, this is how I keep the mould from my brain and find release from Fortune's malice. I am content to have her beat me down this way to see if she won't become ashamed.

At nightfall I return home and enter my study. There on the threshold I remove my dirty, mud-spattered clothes, slip on my regal and courtly robes, and thus fittingly attired, I enter the ancient courts of bygone men where, having received a friendly welcome, I feed on the food that is mine alone and that I was born for. I am not ashamed to speak with them and inquire into the reasons for their actions; and they answer me in kindly fashion. And so for four hours I feel no annoyance; I forget all troubles; poverty holds no fears, and death loses its terrors. I become entirely one of them. And since Dante says that there can be no knowledge without retention, I have set down what I have gained from their conversations and composed a little book, *De Principatibus*, in which I probe as deeply as I can . . . into the subject, discussing what a principality is, what kinds there are, how they are won, how they are maintained, and why they are lost. If ever any trifle of mine has pleased you, this one should not displease you; and to a prince—especially a new prince—it ought to be welcome. Therefore I am addressing it to the Magnificent Giuliano [de' Medici]. . . .

I am going to waste. I cannot go on this way for long without becoming contemptible in my poverty. Besides, there is my wish that these Medici lords would begin to use me, even if they were to start by setting me to roll a stone, for if I should then fail to win their confidence I could only blame myself. Having read this thing, one will see that I did not sleep or gamble away the fifteen years I was engaged in the study of statecraft, and anyone ought to value the services of a man who has become richly experienced at another's expense. As to my loyalty, there should be no doubt, for having always kept faith, I am not about to begin breaking it now. Anyone who has been faithful and true as I have been for forty-three years can hardly change his nature, and my poverty is witness to my honesty and goodness. . . .

The letter is dated December 10, 1513, and this is the first mention of *The Prince*. There is really no need to look further for

Machiavelli's motive in writing it. Yet this motive has not always been fully understood. Some critics, recalling Machiavelli's republican sympathies and his long service to Soderini's government, have attributed the work to crass opportunism and have charged the writer with hypocrisy. Such a view is, to say the least, an oversimplification. It overlooks the spirit of the book and tends to falsify the political temper of the times. If we assume that Machiavelli chose to play the devil's advocate merely to get a job, we will miss the warmth of feeling that informs his pages, for underneath the crisp and chilling logic the thought often glows with indignation, with hope that is wrung from despair and defies logic. Far from being a brilliant exercise in opportunism, *The Prince* is a desperate effort to find a remedy for the wretched conditions into which his country had fallen. "I love my country more than my soul," Machiavelli wrote, and *The Prince* reflects this.

To be sure, poverty and idleness weighed on him. But politics was his life, "the food that is mine alone," he says, "and that I was born for." For him to be cut off from political activity was like being deprived of vital air. The degree to which he was possessed by this *furor politicus* should be gauged not so much by his large body of writings on the subject as by the high place political matters held in his scheme of values. Surely nothing stood higher. And this helps to explain how he came to his major political discovery.

Machiavelli's chief contribution to political thought lies in his freeing political action from moral considerations. For him, the political imperative was essentially unrelated to the ethical imperative. This is not to say that he was an advocate of immorality. There is ample evidence, in fact, that he held moral views which, by and large, coincided with those of his contemporaries. But where political theorists had traditionally built their ideas upon theological and ethical foundations, judging institutions and rulers against a pattern of what ought to be, Machiavelli affirmed that religion and morals had no place in the political arena except insofar as they served political ends. For him, the value of an institution or a ruler was to be determined only by practical success, and, at least as far as *The*

Prince is concerned, success meant the acquisition and preservation of political power. He regarded the ideas of his predecessors as mere "fancies." ". . . I depart from the rules set down by others," he tells us in Chapter 15. "But since it is my intention to write something of use . . . , I deem it best to stick to the practical truth of things rather than to fancies. Many men have imagined republics and principalities that never really existed at all. Yet the way men live is so far removed from the way they ought to live that anyone who abandons what is for what should be pursues his downfall rather than his preservation."

To be sure, history is replete with examples of rulers who, long before Machiavelli appeared, had often acted without any regard for ethical imperatives. But it remained for Machiavelli to affirm that such actions were in accord with the legitimate principles of political conduct. Without any theoretical sanction, these men had not scrupled to predicate their actions upon purely political criteria. Machiavelli provided the sanction their deeds—and those of subsequent rulers—required by declaring in effect that if statecraft was to be practiced successfully, conventional morality had to be set aside and replaced by what later writers were to call "reasons of state." Thus he established a cleavage between political conduct and personal morality—a cleavage that haunts the conscience of men even to this day.

The modern reader should guard against the error of reading *The Prince* as though its author had been aware of philosophical and doctrinal systems relating to the state and society that had no existence in his time. Unless he does so, he will seek for answers to questions Machiavelli never considered. Indeed, it is important to remember that Machiavelli was not a systematic thinker. He was not concerned with the problem of rationalizing a complete and coherent political theory. His aim in *The Prince* was to describe the rules of power politics based upon his analysis of history—an analysis which, whatever its shortcomings, marked a long step forward in making sense out of the welter of conflicting events in his time. It has since helped in making sense out of those of subsequent times as well.

One of the most characteristic elements of his thought in this work is its proximity to action. He was not a scholar, and he did not have the temperament of one who finds knowledge an end in itself. Knowledge for him was a springboard for the deed. He doubtless regarded his analysis of men and events as the basis for a program, a blueprint which some likely ruler would take up and build upon. This aim helps to account for the fact that, surprisingly, he does not even pause to define the nature of the state or to develop what its relation to the society living under its laws should be. It also helps to account for his insistence upon logic and his air of scientific objectivity. He must have believed that he was not presenting the opinions of a mere expert, but that he had unlocked the very truth of things and was proclaiming that alone.

The skeptical reader will discover that Machiavelli's argument is neither as logical nor as consistent as it appears, and that the objectivity, though it is not just a pose, is not always real either. He will discover that the work is not purely a synthesis of keen and original deductions from fact. It is also a work of imagination. Where the author's own logic might have led him to despair for his country, his imagination stepped in, metaphor in hand, to reverse the direction of that logic and give life to his hope (a hope which is not fully revealed until the last chapter). Contrary to what some of his critics have said, *The Prince* is not the work of a man whose veins ran ice water. Instead, it is the work of a man who looked out upon the wreckage of history with anguish in his heart and insisted that a solution—not one that would emerge in the fullness of time, but now—could be found. Such a solution would require desperate measures, strength, courage, skill, and favorable circumstances—in two words, *virtù* and *fortuna*.

He must have believed that the man and the moment were at hand when, not long before his letter to Vettori in which he announced *The Prince*, he saw a chance to return to his proper sphere of action—politics. More than that, he saw a chance to play a leading role in the creation of a state based upon his own ideas—a state large and strong enough to be feared by its neighbors and to serve as a bulwark against foreign incursions.

For he had got wind that Pope Leo X was planning to carve out a state for one of his nephews, either Giuliano or Lorenzo de' Medici. Thus, perhaps in July, 1513, he set himself to write *The Prince*. Working in haste, he probably completed it by the following December, since he stated in the letter to Vettori quoted above that it only needed to be "fattened and polished."

But *The Prince*, as we have it, does not show any great labor of the file, and this, strangely, is one of its virtues. Free of rhetorical flourishes, the style lays bare the mind at work, a mind impatient of all nuances and shadings of thought, but poised for irony and quick with sarcasm. Lively and ductile, it is irresistibly attracted to sharp antitheses, aphorisms, and half-concealed images. The pace is hurried, and indeed at times the writer's pen seems in danger of losing its battle to keep up with the headlong rush of ideas as clause follows upon clause. As a consequence, the syntax does not always flow smoothly, and even the grammar becomes shaky. Yet these are only minor flaws. Lacking grace, the expression nevertheless remains lucid, even if we sometimes wish that the diction were more precise and the pace more restrained. Whenever possible, the writer adheres to a simple pattern: every argument unfolds a lesson and comes to rest upon a political axiom, often new and always, in his view, incontrovertible. All in all, the style is in accord with the shape and temper of Machiavelli's thought.

But there is an appeal to the book that goes beyond the brilliance of its ideas and the vigor of its style. Time has dimmed some of the sparkle of its originality, and the modern reader is obliged to summon his historical imagination if he is to recapture the sense of shock and novelty which Machiavelli's first readers experienced. But time has not dimmed its direct and uncompromising honesty, its almost ruthless avoidance of every form of cant. Here there is no bowing to pious clichés, to pretended sensibilities, or hallowed euphemisms. Seldom has a writer done so little to ease the way for his ideas. And one may wonder, in fact, whether those who have reacted to Machiavelli with such voluble horror have not been more shocked by his candor than by the character of the ruler he describes.

On the whole, *The Discourses Upon the First Ten Books of*

Titus Livy is another matter. As already suggested, this is the work in which Machiavelli fully reveals those republican sympathies that have led some critics to doubt his sincerity in *The Prince* (but in fact the same sympathies are more than hinted at there). Though the question cannot be discussed here at length, certain differences of aim which, incidentally, help to bridge the irreconcilable gulf between the two works should be mentioned. *The Prince* was intended to provide a drastic solution to contemporary political ills. *The Discourses*, on the other hand, was intended to provide an evaluation of the institutions of republican Rome, institutions which Machiavelli—typical man of the Renaissance that he was—tended to idealize. Moreover, the one focuses upon the means of acquiring or founding a state, while the other focuses upon the means of preserving it. It may be that Machiavelli saw the program he set down in *The Prince* as a necessary preliminary step to the ultimate establishment of the republican state he favored. But it may be also that he thought the society of his day—very different from that of ancient Rome—was too soft and corrupt to sustain the sort of government he really desired. Yet it cannot be denied that *The Discourses* presents a far more generous view of human nature than does *The Prince*, even though the same ideas concerning the relation of personal morality to political morality appear in both. The "hero" of *The Prince*, it must be remembered, is a ruthless despot, while the "hero" of *The Discourses* is the people of ancient Rome—"my Romans," as Machiavelli called them.

Not long after beginning *The Discourses*, Machiavelli set them aside to write *The Prince* for reasons already mentioned; then he took up *The Discourses* again and continued to make additions until about 1519. He seems to have been in no hurry to finish them. This is evident from their more leisurely pace, their more casual organization, and their rather frequent repetitions of argument.

The individual selections from that lengthy work which appear in this volume were chosen primarily on the basis of two criteria—for their representative qualities and for the contrasts they provide to the ideas developed in *The Prince*. Those dealing largely with military problems, however, have been omitted entirely, since they are not likely to be of interest to the modern reader. On the other hand, representative discourses setting forth Machiavelli's views concerning religion and his views concerning republics have been included. Thus the volume may fairly claim to include all that is vital and characteristic in Machiavelli's political thought.

In making this translation, accuracy has been the primary objective, but I have also sought to preserve Machiavelli's mode of expression insofar as the demands of fidelity and clarity allowed. For the Italian text I have used the edition of Mario Bonfantini (Niccolò Machiavelli: *Opere*, Milano, 1954). It bears repeating that Machiavelli's ideas grew directly out of his consideration of specific historical events, and for that reason the reader must know what those events were. The Notes aim primarily to satisfy that need.

Daniel Donno

The Prince

T HOSE WHO wish to win favor with a prince customarily offer him those things which they hold most precious or which they see him most delight in. Very often, therefore, we see princes presented with horses, weapons, cloth of gold, precious gems, or similar ornaments worthy of their greatness. Wishing, then, to present myself to Your Highness with some mark of my duty to you, I have been unable to find anything I possess that I hold so dear or esteem so highly as my knowledge of the actions of great men, learned from long experience in modern affairs and from constant reading of ancient ones. Having long examined and reflected upon these matters with great diligence and having now set them down in a small volume, I send it to Your Highness. Though I judge this work unworthy to be presented to you, nevertheless, I am very confident that, because of your benevolence, you will accept it, considering that there can come no greater gift from me than the means to understand in a very short time all that which I, after many years, through many labors and dangers, have come to know and understand. I have not adorned this work with fine phrases, with swelling, pompous words, or with any of those blandishments or external ornaments with which many set forth and decorate their matter. For I have chosen either that nothing at all should bring it honor or that the variety of its material and the gravity of its subject matter alone should make it welcome. Nor do I wish it thought a presumption that a man of low and poor estate dare consider and set forth regulations for the rule of princes. For as those who draw landscapes set themselves on the plain to examine the character of hills and of high places and set themselves on the summits to examine the lowlands, so in order thoroughly to understand the nature of the populace

one must be a prince, and in order thoroughly to understand
the nature of a prince one must be of the people. Therefore,
may Your Highness accept this little gift in the spirit with
which I send it. If you will diligently read and consider it, you
will detect in it one of my deepest desires, which is that you
will come to that greatness which fortune and your own qualities promise you. And if from your great height Your Highness
will sometimes cast a glance below to these lowly places, you
will see how undeservedly I endure the heavy and relentless
malice of fortune.[2]

CHAPTER 1

The Kinds of Principalities and the Means
by Which They Are Acquired

ALL STATES and all dominions that hold and have held
power over men have been and are either republics or
principalities. Principalities are either hereditary, in which case
the family of the ruler has long been in power, or they are new.
The new ones are either entirely new, as Milan was to
Francesco Sforza,[1] or they are, so to speak, members added to
the hereditary possession of the prince who acquires them, as
the Kingdom of Naples is to the King of Spain.[2] The dominions thus acquired have been accustomed either to live under a
prince or to be free; and they are acquired either by fortune or
by ability.[3]

CHAPTER 2

HEREDITARY PRINCIPALITIES

I SHALL exclude any discussion of republics, having discussed them at length elsewhere.[1] I shall consider principalities alone and, following the indicated plan, shall discuss how they may be governed and preserved.

I say, then, that hereditary states accustomed to the family of their ruler are more easily kept than new ones, because it is sufficient if the prince does not abandon the methods of his ancestors and proves adaptable when unforeseen events occur. In this way a prince of ordinary capability will always keep his state unless he is deprived of it by an exceptional or exceedingly powerful force. If he is once deprived of it, however, he will nevertheless regain it at the slightest adversity that the conqueror encounters.

In Italy we have the example of the Duke of Ferrara, who was able to sustain the assaults of the Venetians in 1484 and those of Pope Julius in 1510 for no other reason than that he had been long established in that dominion.[2] The hereditary prince has less cause and less need to offend than a new one. Hence it follows that he is more readily loved. If unusual vices do not make him hated, it is reasonable to suppose that his subjects will feel a natural affection for him. Furthermore, one change always leaves dentations upon which to build another,[3] but in a long and continuous rule the recollection of changes and of their causes tends to be forgotten.

CHAPTER 3

MIXED PRINCIPALITIES

IN A new principality, however, there are difficulties. To begin with, if it is not entirely new, but an added member so to speak (the old and the new together being called a mixed principality), changes of authority come about from a natural hazard which exists in all new principalities: that is, from the willingness of men to change one lord for another, believing thus to improve their lot. For this reason they take arms against their ruler; but in this they deceive themselves, for experience will prove that they will actually have worsened their lot. This in turn will be the result of another common and natural necessity, for by the presence of his soldiers and by those other innumerable offenses that follow upon conquest, the new ruler must inevitably distress those over whom he establishes his rule. So it happens that he makes enemies of all those whom he has injured in occupying the new principality, and yet he cannot keep the friendship of those who have set him up; for he cannot satisfy them as they had expected and, since he is obligated to them, he cannot use strong medicine against them. Even if one has a very strong army, he will always need the good will of the inhabitants when entering a province. For these reasons Louis XII, King of France, quickly occupied Milan and quickly lost it. Ludovico's own forces were enough to take it from him the first time because those people who had opened the gates to the King, finding themselves deceived in their opinions and in their expectations, could not endure the irritations inflicted by their new ruler.[1]

It is indeed true, however, that after one has conquered a rebellious territory a second time, it will be less easily lost, for the ruler, using the rebellion as his excuse, will be the less reluctant to establish himself solidly by punishing defectors, uncovering suspects, and strengthening his position wherever it is weak. Therefore, to have the King of France lose Milan the first time, a Duke Ludovico threatening the borders was sufficient; to lose it a second time, the opposition of the whole world, together with the defeat and the expulsion of the King's army from Italy, was needed.[2] This came about for the above-mentioned reasons. Nevertheless, he did lose it both the first and second time. The general reasons for the first loss have been treated. It remains to speak of the second, and to consider what remedies the King of France had and did not use, and what remedies another in the same situation could have availed himself of in order to keep such a conquest.

I say, therefore, that these conquered states which are joined to a state already long held by the conqueror may either belong to the same region and have the same language, or they may not. When they do, it is very easy to keep them, especially if they are not accustomed to freedom. To hold them securely, it is enough to have extinguished the line of princes who ruled them formerly and to maintain the pre-existent conditions. When there is no distinction of custom, men will live quietly, as happened in Burgundy, Brittany, Gascony, and Normandy, which have long been a part of France. Though there is some distinction of language among them, the customs are nevertheless alike, and the people can easily get along with each other. Anyone who conquers such territories and wishes to hold on to them must do two things: the first is to extinguish the ruling family; the second is to alter neither the laws nor the taxes. Thus in a short time they will become one with the conqueror's original possessions.

But when one acquires states in a province where the language, the customs, and the laws are different, there are difficulties; here both fortune and great ability are needed to keep them. One of the best and most ready solutions is for the new ruler to reside there. This expedient would make the new possession safer and more lasting, as it did for the Turk in the case of Greece.[3] Despite all other measures taken to hold that state, he would have been unable to keep it unless he had gone there to live. Being on the spot, one may observe disorders as they arise and quell them quickly; not being present, one will learn about them only when they have assumed such proportions that they cannot be quelled. Moreover, the new province is not despoiled by the ruler's officials. The subjects are satisfied that they have ready recourse to the prince. Consequently, they have more reason to love him if they choose to be good, and more reason to fear him if they choose to behave otherwise. A foreign enemy, thinking of attacking such a state, would be likely to show more respect, for a resident prince could only be defeated with great difficulty.

The next best solution is to send colonies to one or two places which could serve to shackle that state. It is necessary either to do this or to keep a large force of cavalry and infantry there. Colonies do not cost much. Without expense, or with little, they may be sent out and maintained, and they will harm only those whose fields and houses they appropriate for their own use—a minimal part of the population. Those who are harmed, being dispersed and poor, can cause no trouble. All the rest, on the one hand, will be left unharmed (and hence should remain quiet); and, on the other hand, will be fearful lest by some wrongdoing the same that happened to those who were deprived should happen to them. To conclude, such colonies are not costly, are very loyal, and do little harm; those who are hurt, as already indicated, cannot annoy because they are poor and dispersed. At this point one may note that men must be either pampered or annihilated. They avenge light offenses; they cannot avenge severe ones; hence, the harm one does to a man must be such as to obviate any fear of revenge. In any case, by maintaining soldiers instead of colonies, a prince will spend much more, since he will have to use the entire revenue of the state to protect it. Thus the acquisition will become a loss. This method is also more harmful because it annoys the entire state as the troops are moved from one lodging to another. Everyone will feel the disruption and become an enemy—an enemy who can be troublesome because, though beaten, he is ever at home. From every point of view, therefore, this kind of protection is just as useless as colonies are useful.

Moreover, a prince who occupies a province which, as previously described, differs from his own, must become the leader and defender of the less powerful neighboring states and

seek to weaken the more powerful among them. He must also
be on guard lest by any chance some foreigner equal to him in
power should enter them. Such an event always comes about
through the help of discontented inhabitants who willingly admit a foreign power either through excessive ambition or
through fear, as was the case with the Etolians, who admitted
the Romans into Greece.[4] So it was also with every province
that the Romans entered: they were brought in by the inhabitants themselves. It is in the nature of things that as soon as a
powerful foreigner enters a province, all the weaker powers in
it will become his allies through envy of those who have been
ruling over them. This is so true that, with respect to minor
powers, the invader need do nothing at all to win them, for they
will all willingly merge in the state which he has acquired. He
has but to see to it that they do not gain too much strength and
authority. With his own forces and their support, he can very
early reduce the stronger powers and then become arbiter of
the entire province. Any ruler who does not succeed in doing
this will soon lose what he has won, or so long as he does manage to hold it, will have a host of difficulties and annoyances.
The Romans very carefully observed this policy in the
provinces they conquered. They sent out colonies; they protected the lesser powers without increasing their strength; they
reduced those who were strong, and they did not permit powerful foreigners to gain a footing. Their conduct in Greece will
suffice as an example: there the Romans protected the
Achaeans and the Etolians, reduced the kingdom of the
Macedonians, and expelled Antiochus. Nor did they ever reward the Achaeans and the Etolians by allowing them to enlarge their states, or allow Philip to persuade them to become
his friends until they had weakened him.[5] Nor did the power of
Antiochus ever induce them to permit his keeping any part of
Greece. In this instance the Romans did everything that wise
princes should do who must have regard not only for existing
disorders but for future ones as well, avoiding them with all
possible diligence. By making provision in advance, princes
may easily avoid such difficulties; but if they wait until they
are near at hand, the medicine will not be in time, for by then

the malady will have become incurable. In this matter the situation is the same as physicians report concerning hectic fever: in the beginning the disease is easy to cure but hard to diagnose; with the passage of time, having gone unrecognized and unmedicated, it becomes easy to diagnose but hard to cure. So it is with a state: when ills are recognized in advance (and only the prudent can do this), they are quickly cured. But when, having gone unrecognized, they are allowed to increase until everyone may recognize them, then remedy is no longer possible.

Thus the Romans, foreseeing difficulties, always remedied them. And they never allowed them to persist in order to avoid a war, for they knew that wars cannot be avoided and can only be deferred to the advantage of others. Therefore they chose to go to war against Philip and Antiochus in Greece in order to avoid having to deal with them in Italy. For the time, they could have avoided both dangers, but they chose not to. Nor were they ever pleased with the sort of advice that is always on the lips of our present-day wise men: that is, to enjoy the benefits of time.[6] Instead, they were pleased to use their strength and prudence. For time bears all things out and may produce good as readily as evil, evil as readily as good.

But let us turn to France and consider whether she has done any of the things mentioned; and I will speak not of Charles but of Louis.[7] Since Louis held possessions in Italy for a longer time, it is easier to examine his proceedings; and you will see that he did the contrary of what one should do in order to hold power in a state different from one's own.

King Louis was brought into Italy through the ambitions of the Venetians, who hoped by his coming to gain half of Lombardy.[8] I do not mean to censure King Louis's decision in this matter, for having chosen to set foot in Italy and having no friends here—indeed, all gates being closed against him because of King Charles's conduct[9]—he was compelled to accept what friendship he could. This wise plan would have succeeded if he had not made errors in other matters. Having taken Lombardy, he quickly regained all the influence which Charles had lost: Genoa submitted, the Florentines became his allies;

the Marquis of Mantua, the Duke of Ferrara, the Bentivogli, the Countess of Forlì, the Lords of Faenza, Pesaro, Rimini, Camerino, and Piombino, the Lucchese, Pisans, and Sienese—all came forward to offer their friendship. The Venetians could then wonder at the rashness of their decision. To acquire a couple of towns in Lombardy, they had made King Louis master over a third of Italy.

Let us now consider how easily the King could have preserved his influence in Italy if he had followed the rules set forth above and protected all his friends who, since they were numerous and weak and afraid—some of the Church, others of the Venetians—were compelled to stay loyal to him. By keeping their support, he could easily have been secure against those who remained strong. But scarcely had he gained Milan when he did the contrary in assisting Pope Alexander to occupy Romagna.[10] And he did not realize that in taking this step he was making himself weak by casting off his friends and those who had leaped to his protection, while he was making the Church strong by adding temporal power to the spiritual power which gives it so much authority. Having made an initial error, he was obliged to make still others. Indeed, to put an end to Pope Alexander's ambitions, and to prevent his becoming lord of Tuscany he was forced to come into Italy himself.[11] Nor did it suffice him to have strengthened the Church and cast off his friends. In order to gain Naples, he divided it with the King of Spain.[12] Thus, whereas he had been sole arbiter of Italy, he now brought in a partner, so that all those who had ambitions and were displeased with him could have someone to turn to. And whereas he could have left a king in Naples who would have been his pensionary, he removed him in order to install one who could remove the French king himself.[13]

It is truly a natural and ordinary thing to desire gain; and when those who can succeed attempt it, they will always be praised and not blamed. But if they cannot succeed, yet try anyway, they are guilty of error and are blameworthy. Therefore, if France with her own forces could have attacked Naples, she should have done so; if not, she should not have partitioned it. If she is to be excused for having partitioned Lombardy with the

Venetians because she thereby gained a foothold in Italy, this second partitioning merits censure since it cannot be excused by the same necessity.

Louis thus made these five mistakes: he extinguished the weaker powers; he strengthened one that was already strong in Italy; he brought in a most potent foreign power;[14] he did not come and reside here; and he failed to establish colonies.

Yet these errors could not have hurt him while he lived if he had not committed a sixth, that of reducing the power of Venice.[15] If he had not strengthened the Church nor brought the power of Spain into Italy, it would have been reasonable and necessary to reduce her; but having taken both these actions, he should never have permitted Venice's ruin. For, being strong, Venice could have kept others from venturing into Lombardy, since she would never have agreed to their doing so unless she herself could become mistress there, and no one would have seized it from France merely to yield it to Venice in turn. Moreover, no one would have dared to attack both France and Venice at the same time. If anyone says King Louis ceded Romagna to Pope Alexander and the Kingdom of Naples to Spain to avoid a war, I answer with the reasons set forth above—that one should never permit a disorder to persist in order to avoid a war, for war is not avoided thereby but merely deferred to one's own disadvantage. And if others allege the reason for this to have been the promise Louis made to the Pope to undertake the invasion of Romagna in exchange for the dissolution of his marriage and a cardinal's cap for Rouen, I reply with what I shall set forth below concerning the promises of princes and how they ought to be kept.

King Louis, therefore, lost Lombardy because he failed to observe any of those rules observed by others who, having conquered provinces, chose to keep them. Nor is this to be wondered at, but is very ordinary and reasonable. I spoke about this matter with the Cardinal of Rouen at Nantes when Valentino (for so Cesare Borgia, the son of Pope Alexander, was popularly called) occupied Romagna. When the Cardinal of Rouen told me that the Italians did not understand war, I answered that the French did not understand politics; for if they had understood, they would not have allowed the Church to gain so much in power. And experience has shown that the greatness both of the Church and of Spain in Italy was brought about by France, while France's ruin was, in turn, brought about by them. From this we may extract a general rule which scarcely ever fails: He who causes another to become powerful ruins himself, for he brings such a power into being either by design or by force, and both of these elements are suspect to the one whom he has made powerful.

CHAPTER 4

WHY ALEXANDER'S SUCCESSORS WERE ABLE
TO KEEP POSSESSION OF DARIUS' KINGDOM
AFTER ALEXANDER'S DEATH

CONSIDERING THE difficulties involved in keeping a newly acquired state, one may wonder how it happened that the Asiatic lands which Alexander the Great conquered in but a few years and occupied only briefly before his death did not rebel, as might have been expected.[1] Yet the fact is that his successors did manage to hold on to them, and had no difficulty doing so except such as arose among themselves through personal ambition.[2] The answer is that all principalities for which some record exists have been ruled in two different ways: either by a single prince aided by servants functioning as ministers and governing by his favor and concession; or by a prince with barons holding title not by his grace but by right of inheritance. The barons have dominions and subjects of their own who are bound to them by natural affections and regard them as their lords. In states which are governed by a prince and his servants, the prince has greater authority because no one in his land recognizes anyone but him as master. And if anyone does give obedience to another, he only does so as to a minister for whom he feels no tie of affection.

Examples of these two ways of governing in our day are Turkey and France. The whole Kingdom of Turkey is governed by one man; everyone else is his servant. Having divided his kingdom into sanjaks,[3] the monarch sends various administrators out to them, shifting them about and replacing them as he pleases. But the King of France is surrounded by a large number of lords of ancient lineage who are recognized and loved by their subjects. They have their degrees of preeminence, which the king cannot deprive them of without danger to himself. Anyone who considers both these states, therefore, will note that there would be difficulty in conquering the kingdom of the Turks, but ease in keeping it once it was conquered. He will note, on the other hand, that the Kingdom of France in some respects would be easier to occupy but more difficult to hold.

The difficulty of occupying the kingdom of the Turks arises from the fact that there is no possibility of being called in by princes of that kingdom and no hope of being assisted by a revolt on the part of those surrounding the ruler. This is the consequence of the above-mentioned factors. For since all such persons are servants and dependents of their ruler, they can be corrupted only with great difficulty; and even if they were corrupted they would prove of little use because, for reasons already given, they would be unable to draw the populace after them. Anyone who attacks the Turks must, therefore, expect to find them entirely united, and would do well to rely upon his own forces rather than upon the disorder of the enemy. But if the Turk were beaten in the field and were so thoroughly routed that he could not reassemble his armies, there would be no cause for concern except for the family of the ruler; and if this were extinguished, there would be no one left to fear at all, since any others would have no standing among the people. Even as the conqueror could not rely upon them before his victory, so he need not fear them after it.

The contrary is true in monarchies governed as France is,

for you can enter them with ease by winning over one of the barons of the kingdom, since malcontents and others who desire a change can always be found. For the reasons stated, such persons can open the way for you and facilitate your victory. But in preserving it afterward infinite difficulties will arise in regard to both those who have helped you and those whom you have oppressed. Nor will it suffice to extinguish the ruler's family, for nobles capable of mounting new insurrections will remain. Unable either to please them or to annihilate them, you will lose the state at the first likely opportunity.

Now, if you consider the nature of Darius' government you will find it similar to that of the Turkish monarchy. Therefore it was necessary that Alexander make an all-out attack and deprive Darius of the field. After this victory, Darius then being dead, the state remained securely in Alexander's hands, for the reasons already given. And his successors, had they remained united, could have enjoyed it in ease. Nor did any tumults arise in that kingdom except those which they themselves caused. But it is not so easy to keep possession of states which are organized as France is. This explains how it happened that there were so many insurrections against the Romans in Spain, France, and Greece resulting from the numerous principalities into which those states had been divided.[4] As long as the memory of these principalities survived, the Romans remained insecure in their possessions. Not until the enduring power of the empire had effaced all memory of them did the Romans become safely entrenched. Thereafter, even when fighting among themselves, each of the Roman leaders was able to gain the support of some part of these provinces, according to the degree of authority he held in them; and once the line of the ancestral rulers had become extinct, the people recognized none but Romans as their masters. Therefore, all these things having been considered, no one should marvel at the ease with which Alexander kept possession of Asia or at the difficulties which others, like Pyrrhus and many more, had in preserving their conquests.[5] The difference does not arise from the greater or lesser ability of the conqueror, but from dissimilarities in the conquered lands.

CHAPTER 5

How to Govern Cities and Principalities That, Prior to
Being Occupied, Lived Under Their Own Laws

WHEN A state accustomed to live in freedom under its
own laws is acquired, there are three ways of keeping
it: the first is to destroy it;[1] the second is to go to live there in
person; the third is to let it continue to live under its own laws,
taking tribute from it, and setting up a government composed
of a few men who will keep it friendly to you. Such a government, being the creature of the prince, will be aware that it cannot survive without his friendship and support, and it will do
everything to maintain his authority. A city which is used to
freedom is more easily controlled by means of its own citizens
than by any other, provided one chooses not to destroy it.

Take, for example, the Spartans and the Romans. The
Spartans held Athens and Thebes by setting up a government
of a few men in each; nevertheless they lost both.[2] In order to
hold on to Capua, Carthage, and Numantia, the Romans destroyed them; yet they did not lose them.[3] They hoped to hold
Greece in almost the same way as the Spartans had done, leaving her free under her own laws; yet they were not successful,
and so they were compelled to destroy many cities of that
province in order to keep possession of it.[4]

For in truth there is no sure method of holding such cities
except by destruction. Anyone who becomes master of a city
accustomed to freedom and does not destroy it may expect to
be destroyed by it; for such a city may always justify rebellion
in the name of liberty and its ancient institutions. These are not
forgotten either through passage of time or through benefits received. Despite any actions or provisions one may take, if the
inhabitants are not divided and dispersed, they will not forget
that name and those institutions, and they will quickly have recourse to them at every chance, as Pisa did after a hundred
years of servitude under the Florentines.[5]

But when cities or provinces have been accustomed to live

under a prince and his line becomes extinct, being on the one hand used to obeying and on the other deprived of their leader, they cannot agree among themselves in the selection of a new one and do not know how to live in freedom. Hence they are slower to take up arms, and a prince may more easily win them and hold them. But in republics there is greater vigor, greater hatred, greater desire for revenge, and the memory of earlier freedom cannot and will not let them rest. Thus, the surest procedure is either to destroy them or to live in them.

CHAPTER 6

CONCERNING NEW PRINCIPALITIES ACQUIRED BY ONE'S OWN ARMS AND ABILITY

LET NO one wonder if in the discussion that follows concerning new princes in newly established states I shall set forth some very outstanding examples. Men almost always walk in paths beaten by others and act by imitation. Though he cannot hold strictly to the ways of others or match the ability of those he imitates, a prudent man must always tread the path of great men and imitate those who have excelled, so that even if his ability does not match theirs, at least he will achieve some semblance of it. He should act like a prudent archer who, knowing the limitation of his bow and judging the target to be too far off, sets his aim still farther off, not to strike so distant a mark, but rather to strike the desired target through the more ambitious aim.

I say, therefore, that the degree of difficulty which a newly risen prince in a newly founded state encounters will depend upon the degree of ability he possesses. And since his rise from private citizen to prince presupposes either ability or good fortune, it would appear that one or the other of these factors will in part reduce his difficulties.[1] Those who have relied least upon fortune, however, have been the most successful. The prince's difficulties should also be reduced by the fact that, having no other dominions, he will be obliged to live in the new state.

But to come to those who have become princes through ability rather than good fortune, I say that the most outstanding were Moses, Cyrus, Romulus, Theseus, and the like.[2] And though one should not mention Moses, because he was the mere executor of things commanded by God, still he deserves admiration if only for that divine grace which made him worthy to speak with God. But let us consider Cyrus and others who conquered and founded kingdoms. They were all admirable; and if their particular actions and methods are considered, they will not seem discordant with those of Moses, who had so great a Preceptor. Examining their lives and actions, one cannot find that they owed anything to fortune but the opportunity which gave them matter to shape into the form they thought right. Without an opportunity, their abilities would have been wasted, and without their abilities, the opportunity would have arisen in vain.

Therefore it was needful that Moses find the people of Israel enslaved and oppressed by the Egyptians in order that they would be ready to follow him out of Egypt to escape from servitude. It was needful that Romulus be taken out of Alba and exposed at birth in order that he could become King of Rome and founder of that nation. It was needful that Cyrus find the Persians dissatisfied with the rule of the Medes, and find the Medes soft and effeminate as a result of prolonged peace. Theseus would have been unable to display his ability if he had not found the Athenians scattered. These opportunities, then, gave these men the chance they needed, and their great abilities made them recognize it. As a result, their countries were ennobled and made prosperous.

Those who become princes by virtue of their abilities, as these men did, acquire dominion with difficulty but maintain it with ease. The difficulties they encounter in winning their dominions arise in part from the new forms of administration and new methods which they are compelled to introduce in order to establish their state and assure their security. It must be realized that there is nothing more difficult to plan, more uncertain of success, or more dangerous to manage than the establishment of a new order of government; for he who introduces it makes enemies of all those who derived advantage from the old order and finds but lukewarm defenders among those who stand to gain from the new one. Such a lukewarm attitude grows partly out of fear of the adversaries, who have the law on their side, and partly from the incredulity of men in general, who actually have no faith in new things until they have been proved by experience. Hence it happens that whenever those in the enemy camp have a chance to attack, they do so with partisan fervor, while the others defend themselves rather passively, so that both they and the prince are endangered.

To treat the matter thoroughly, however, it is necessary to consider whether such innovators stand on their own or whether they depend upon others; that is, whether in order to fulfill their mission they must plead or can compel. When the first is the case, it always happens that matters turn out badly and they achieve nothing. But when they depend upon their own resources and can use force, they rarely fail. From this it follows that all armed prophets have succeeded and all unarmed ones have failed; for in addition to what has already been said, people are by nature changeable. It is easy to persuade them about some particular matter, but it is hard to hold them to that persuasion. Hence it is necessary to provide that when they no longer believe, they can be forced to believe.

Moses, Cyrus, Theseus, and Romulus would have been unable to have their constitutions obeyed for so long a time if they had been unarmed, as was the case in our own day with Fra' Girolamo Savonarola, who failed with his new laws as soon as the multitude no longer believed in them.[3] He had no way to keep them faithful to what they had believed, or to force the unbelievers to believe. Therefore, such men encounter great difficulties; but the dangers arise on their way to power, and they must use their resourcefulness to overcome them. Once they have overcome them, however, and have begun to be venerated and, moreover, have suppressed all those

of their own rank who had been jealous of them, they will remain powerful, secure, honored, and successful.

To such lofty examples I wish to add a lesser one that will
nevertheless share some measure of proportion with them; and
let this suffice for all similar instances. I mean Hiero of
Syracuse.[4] From private citizen, he became Lord of Syracuse.
Yet he owed nothing to fortune but the opportunity, for when
the Syracusans were oppressed, they elected him their captain,
and from that he earned the right to become their ruler. He possessed such remarkable ability that even as a private person it
was said of him that he lacked nothing but a kingdom to be a
king.[5] He destroyed the old militia and established a new one;
he abandoned old alliances and formed new ones. Having his
own soldiers and allies, he was thus able to build as he chose
upon this foundation, so that although he exerted great effort to
achieve his position, it required little to keep it.

CHAPTER 7

CONCERNING NEW PRINCIPALITIES ACQUIRED WITH
THE ARMS AND FORTUNES OF OTHERS

T HOSE WHO rise from private station to become princes
by means of good fortune alone do so with scant effort
but remain so with much toil. They encounter no difficulty on
the way, for they fly to their destinations; and all their difficulties begin when they have alighted. Such cases arise when
someone is given a state either for money or as a favor from
the bestower, as happened to many in the Greek cities of Ionia
and the Hellespont when Darius made them princes so that
they would hold those cities for his glory and security,[1] and as
also happened to those who from private citizens became emperors by corrupting the military.[2]

Such individuals depend entirely upon the will and the fortune—two fickle and unstable things— of those who have installed them. They lack both the knowledge and the means to keep their position. They lack the knowledge because, barring the possibility that they are men of exceptional intelligence and skill, they are unlikely to know how to command, since they have always been private citizens. They lack the means because they have no forces upon whose loyalty and good will they can depend. Moreover, like all things in nature that spring up and grow quickly, states that come hastily into being cannot have proper roots and branches; so the first adverse weather destroys them unless, as I have said, those who so suddenly become princes have the rare ability to learn quickly how to preserve what fortune has dropped in their laps and begin to lay those foundations which others have laid before becoming princes.

With respect to both these ways of becoming a prince— that is, through ability or through fortune—I want to set down two examples that occurred within present memory, namely Francesco Sforza and Cesare Borgia.[3] By suitable means and by his own remarkable ability, Francesco rose from private station to become Duke of Milan, and what he gained with a thousand troubles he preserved with little effort. On the other hand, Cesare Borgia, popularly called Duke Valentino, acquired power through his father's fortunes and lost it through the same means, despite the fact that he exerted every effort and did everything that a prudent and capable man should do to entrench himself in those territories which the arms and fortunes of others had granted him. For, as was said before, if one has unusual ability and does not lay the foundations beforehand, he can lay them afterward, though with trouble for the architect and danger to the edifice. If all of Duke Valentino's operations are considered, therefore, it will be clear that he laid strong foundations for his future power; and I do not think it would be superfluous to discuss them, for I know of no better precept to bestow upon a new prince than that he follow the example of his actions. If his methods proved of no avail he was not to blame, for his failure resulted from the extraordinary and extreme malice of fortune.[4]

Wishing to make his son the Duke great, Alexander VI faced many immediate and future difficulties. He saw first of all that there was no way of making him lord of any state not belonging to the Church, and he saw that if he attempted to bestow any of those belonging to the Church upon him, the Duke of Milan and the Venetians would restrain him because Faenza and Rimini were already under the protection of the Venetians.[5] He saw besides that the military forces of Italy, especially those that could have been useful to him, were in the hands of men who had reason to fear the papal power, and therefore could not be trusted. They were all controlled by the Orsini, the Colonnesi, and their accomplices.[6] Consequently, it was necessary to upset the existing arrangements and, by introducing disorder among the Italian states, acquire secure possession of some of them. This was easy to do, for the Pope saw that the Venetians, moved by other considerations, were arranging to have the French re-enter Italy, a scheme which, far from opposing, he facilitated by dissolving Louis's first marriage.[7]

Thus King Louis came into Italy with the help of the Venetians and the consent of Alexander, and he had scarcely entered Milan before Alexander had from him the forces he needed for his venture in Romagna, which he was allowed to undertake by virtue of the King's great prestige. Having thus acquired Romagna and subdued the Colonnesi,[8] Duke Valentino wanted to secure his conquests and embark upon others, but he found two obstacles in his way: the first concerned the doubtful loyalty of his forces; the second concerned the attitude of France. That is, he feared that the Orsini forces, which he had employed, would deliberately fail him and not only impede further conquest but also deprive him of what he had already gained; and he feared that the King would do the same. With regard to the Orsini forces, he got some indication of their state of mind when, after having seized Faenza, he proceeded to advance upon Bologna and saw them turn cold in the assault.[9] As for the King, the Duke recognized his attitude when, having taken the Duchy of Urbino and launched his attack upon Tuscany, he was made to desist.[10] The Duke thereupon decided he would no longer depend upon the arms and fortunes of others.

The first thing he did then was to undermine the Orsini and Colonna factions in Rome, bringing all their adherents of noble rank into his service by assigning them generous provisions and by honoring them, according to their degree, with military and administrative posts. As a result, in a few months they forgot their former factional ties and became entirely loyal to the Duke. After this, having already dispersed the leaders of the Colonna clan, he sought for a chance to destroy those of the Orsini as well. The chance when it came proved a good one, but his use of it proved even better. For the Orsini, belatedly recognizing that the power of the Duke combined with that of the Church spelled their ruin, called a meeting at La Magione, near Perugia. Out of it came the revolt of Urbino, the disorders of Romagna, and a host of perils for the Duke. But with the help of France he overcame them all.[11]

When he had regained his former standing, he decided that in order to avoid risk he would no longer rely upon France or upon the forces of anyone else.[12] He resorted to deception instead, and he knew so well how to dissimulate that the Orsini clan patched up their differences with him through the mediation of Paolo Orsini, toward whom the Duke extended every courtesy, granting him gifts of money, of robes and horses in order to win his confidence. Such was their folly that it led them into his hands at Senigallia.[13] Having suppressed these leaders and made allies of their followers, the Duke now had the sound foundations he needed for the establishment of his own power, since he controlled all of Romagna and the Duchy of Urbino and, most important of all, had gained the good will of all the inhabitants of Romagna, who were beginning to get a taste of good government.

And since this last achievement is worthy of being noted and imitated, I do not wish to pass it over. After the Duke had conquered Romagna, he saw that it had been ruled by impotent lords who had been more inclined to despoil than to govern their subjects, and who had given more cause for disunity than unity, so that the province was ravaged by brigandage, by feuds, and by violence of every kind. Seeing the need for a sound government that would reduce it to peace and order under his sovereign authority, he appointed for this purpose Messer Remirro de Orca, a cruel and resolute individual, to whom he granted the fullest powers. In a short time this man brought peace and unity to the province, thereby gaining great respect. Later, judging that such excessive power was no longer necessary and fearing that it would arouse hatred, the Duke established a civil tribunal in the center of the province, presided over by an outstanding magistrate with a representative from each city. Recognizing that past severities had generated a measure of hatred against him, he then determined to free himself of all popular suspicion by demonstrating that if there had been any acts of cruelty they had proceeded not from him but from his minister instead. Having found an occasion to do this, one morning he had Remirro's body, cut in two, placed on view in the public square of Cesena with a wooden block and a blood-stained knife resting beside it. The horror of that spectacle gave the people reason to be both shocked and gratified.

But let us turn back to where we left off. I say, then, that when the Duke found himself sufficiently powerful and in part safe from any immediate dangers, because he was armed as he wished to be and had largely eliminated such neighboring forces as might have attacked him, he found that the only remaining obstacle to his further conquests was the King of France who, having belatedly seen his error, would not tolerate them.[14] For this reason he began to seek out new allies and to waver in his relations with the French with respect to their campaign in the Kingdom of Naples where the Spanish were laying siege to Gaeta.[15] His aim was to be free of them, and he would have succeeded if Pope Alexander had not died. This was his conduct concerning matters at hand.

Concerning the future, however, he had first of all to consider whether a new successor to the papacy would be friendly to him and would not attempt to deprive him of what Alexander had given him. On this point he planned to assure his safety in four ways: first, by extinguishing the line of all those lords he had despoiled, so as to deprive the new pope of any chance to use them against him; second, by gaining the allegiance of all the noblemen of Rome, as I said earlier, so as to use them to restrain the new pope; third, by winning over as many members of the College of Cardinals as possible; fourth, by acquiring enough power before Pope Alexander's death so that he himself would be capable of resisting any initial attack made against him by Alexander's successor. Of these four objectives, he had achieved three when Alexander died, while the fourth was just short of fulfillment. For he had slain as many of the lords he had despoiled as he could get hold of, and very few had escaped. He had won over the Roman nobility and could claim a very large portion of the College of Cardinals. As to conquests, he had already laid plans for becoming lord of Tuscany, he had already gained possession of both Perugia and Piombino, and he had become the protector of Pisa.

And as soon as he no longer had to consider the wishes of France (actually this was already the case, for the Spaniards had driven the French out of the Kingdom of Naples under such circumstances that both France and Spain needed his friendship), he intended to sweep into Pisa. After this, Lucca and Siena would have quickly surrendered, partly through envy of the Florentines, partly through fear. Then the Florentines would have been helpless. If he had succeeded in this venture (and he would have succeeded the very year Alexander died), he would have been able to manage for himself, relying no longer upon the fortunes and arms of others, but upon his own powers and ability instead. But Alexander died only five years after the Duke had first drawn his sword. He was left with only the province of Romagna consolidated, with everything else still up in the air, standing between two very powerful armies, and deathly ill besides.[16]

Yet the Duke was endowed with so much fierceness of spirit, so much ability, so much knowledge of how men are won or ruined, and had so quickly laid down such firm foundations that if he had not been pressed by the two armies and had been in good health he would have prevailed over every difficulty. That his foundations were sound is clear from the fact that Romagna waited more than a month for him to appear and that, although only half alive, he could remain in Rome without danger. Even when the Baglioni, the Vitelli, and the Orsini came to Rome,[17] they could not raise a force to attack him. Though he could not get his candidate elected pope, still he could prevent anyone he did not want from being elected.[18] But if he had been in good health when Alexander died everything would have been easy for him. He told me when Pope Julius II was elected that he had foreseen everything that could happen at the time of his father's death and had found a remedy for every contingency, but he had never expected that at the same time he too would be near death.

Having reviewed all the Duke's actions, then, I see nothing to blame him for. Indeed, I think he should be proposed—as in fact I have—as an example to be imitated by all those who have come to power through the fortunes and arms of others. Being of great spirit and lofty ambition, he would have been unable to act in any other way. Only the suddenness of Alexander's death coupled with his own illness thwarted his designs. Therefore, if you are a prince in possession of a newly acquired state and deem it necessary to guard against your enemies, to gain allies, to win either by force or fraud, to be loved and feared by your subjects, to be respected and obeyed by your troops, to annihilate those who can or must attack you, to reform and modernize old institutions, to be severe yet cordial, magnanimous and liberal, to abolish a disloyal militia and create a new one, to preserve the friendship of kings and princes in such a way that they will either favor you graciously or oppose you cautiously—then for such purposes you will not find fresher examples to follow than the actions of this man.

Only the election of Julius II to the papacy, in which he made the wrong choice, can be charged against him; for, as I have said, though he could not have had his own choice ratified, he still could have prevented the election of anyone he did not favor. Therefore, he should never have permitted any cardinal he had injured or any who would afterward have cause to fear him to be elected pope, for men do harm either because of fear or because of hatred. Among the cardinals he had injured were Giuliano della Rovere, Giovanni Colonna, Raffaello Riario of Savona, and Ascanio Sforza;[19] and all the others would have had reason to fear him except the Spanish cardinals and the Cardinal of Rouen—the former because of family ties and other obligations, the latter because of his connections with the French kingdom. The Duke, therefore, should have favored the election of a Spaniard above all else and, failing that, he should have accepted the Cardinal of Rouen, not Giuliano della Rovere. Those who believe that where great personages are concerned new favors cause old injuries to be forgotten deceive themselves. Thus the Duke erred in the election, and it was the cause of his downfall.

CHAPTER 8

CONCERNING THOSE WHO BECOME PRINCES BY EVIL MEANS

B UT SINCE a private citizen may also become a prince in two ways which cannot be entirely attributed to fortune or to ability, I do not think these should be overlooked, even though one of them could be treated more extensively in a discussion concerning republics.[1] These two ways relate to occasions when a person ascends to power by wicked and nefarious means, and to occasions when a private citizen becomes the ruler of his country through the wishes of his fellow citizens. The first I will illustrate with two examples (one ancient, the other modern) without otherwise entering into a discussion of its merits, for I think that it would be enough to imitate these examples if one were constrained by necessity to do so.

Not merely from a private calling, but from an abject and lowly one as well, Agathocles of Sicily became King of Syracuse.[2] Born the son of a potter, this man lived wickedly at every stage of his life. Yet his wickedness was accompanied by so much vigor of mind and body that, having taken up a military career, he was able to rise through the ranks and become the commanding officer. Once established in this position, he decided to become Lord of Syracuse and to retain by violence, without obligation to anyone, the power that others had conferred upon him. Having come to an accord on the matter with Hamilcar of Carthage, who was then commanding an army in Sicily, he ordered the Senate and the people of Syracuse to assemble one morning as if affairs of concern to the republic had to be considered. Then, at a given signal, he had his soldiers fall upon all the senators and all the richest citizens. These having been slain, he seized the lordship of the city and held it without any civil opposition. And though he was twice routed by the Carthaginians and even besieged by them, he not only defended his city but, leaving part of his forces behind for its protection, with the others he even invaded Africa and thus freed Syracuse from the siege, reducing the Carthaginians to such extremities that they were compelled to settle for possession of Africa and leave Sicily to him.

Anyone who examines the life and actions of this man, therefore, will find little or nothing to attribute to fortune; for as was said before, it was not through anyone's favor, but rather through his own advancement in the ranks of the army, won at the cost of a thousand hardships and risks, that he gained the power which he then maintained by many bold and hazardous undertakings. Still it cannot be called virtue to slay one's fellow citizens, to betray one's friends, to act without faith, without pity, without religion. By such methods one may win dominion but not glory. But if we consider Agathocles' boldness in confronting and surmounting dangers and his greatness of spirit in enduring and overcoming adversities, we cannot see why he should be judged inferior to any truly outstanding captain. Yet his savage and inhuman cruelty and his many acts of wickedness do not permit him to be celebrated among men of unusual excellence. And that which he accomplished without fortune and without virtue cannot be attributed to either of these qualities.

In our own time, when Pope Alexander VI was still reigning, there was the example of Oliverotto da Fermo.[3] An orphan from childhood, he was raised by Giovanni Fogliani, his maternal uncle, and then in early youth was sent to serve as a soldier under Paolo Vitelli so that by becoming expert in that profession he might attain a worthy rank. After Paolo's death, he served under Paolo's brother Vitellozzo and, being clever, vigorous, and bold, he soon became his chief officer. Deeming it servile, however, to take orders from others, he plotted with certain citizens of Fermo, to whom the enslavement of their city was dearer than its freedom, and with the help of Vitellozzo he resolved to seize the city for himself. He wrote to Giovanni Fogliani, therefore, and said that as he had been away from home for some years, he now desired to visit his uncle and his native city and to look over his inheritance; and since he had toiled for no other purpose but to win honor, he now wanted his fellow citizens to see that he had not wasted his time. Therefore he asked that he be permitted to come honorably escorted by a hundred horsemen, his friends and servants, and that his uncle be pleased to arrange for the citizens of Fermo to give him a worthy reception. Such a welcome, he said, would bring honor not only to himself but to Giovanni as well, since he had been Giovanni's pupil.

Giovanni did not fail in any courteous obligation to his nephew. Having seen to it that the citizens of Fermo received him honorably, he gave him lodgings in his own residence, where a few days later, after having made all necessary arrangements for the crime he contemplated, Oliverotto prepared a sumptuous banquet to which Giovanni Fogliani and all the leading citizens of Fermo had been invited. When the dinner and all the entertainments that are a customary part of such gatherings had come to an end, Oliverotto, as a ruse, launched upon a discussion of certain serious matters and talked of the greatness of Alexander VI and of his son Cesare and of their enterprises. When Giovanni and the others began to reply, Oliverotto rose up suddenly and said that such matters should be discussed in a more private place. He thereupon withdrew into another room with Giovanni and his other guests, but they were scarcely seated when soldiers rushed out from certain hiding places and slew Giovanni and all who were with him.

After the slaughter, Oliverotto mounted his horse, rode through the city and laid siege to the palace of the chief magistrates, who were constrained by fear to obey him, and set up a government at the head of which he placed himself. Having slain all those who could have turned resentment into injury, he proceeded to fortify his position with new civic and military ordinances, so that during the one year in which he ruled he succeeded not only in making himself secure in Fermo but also in becoming a source of anxiety to his neighbors. And, as in the case of Agathocles, his expulsion would have been difficult if he had not allowed himself to be deceived by Cesare Borgia at Senigallia, where, as before mentioned, one year after the parricide he was seized with Vitelli and the Orsini, and there, together with Vitellozzo, who had taught him both valor and perfidy, he was strangled.

Some may wonder how it happened that Agathocles and others like him could so long remain secure in their dominions after their countless acts of cruelty and treachery, and could defend themselves from foreign foes without ever being conspired against by the citizenry, while other men who also resorted to cruelty were unable to keep their states even in times of peace, not to mention the more uncertain times of war. I believe this is explained by proper and improper use of cruelty. It can be said to be properly used (if one may speak favorably of what is bad) when one resorts to it at one stroke out of a need for safety and does not thereafter insist upon it, but seeks instead to replace it with measures that are of the greatest possible use to his subjects. It is improperly used when, though rarely applied at the start, it is resorted to with increasing rather than decreasing frequency as time goes by. Those who follow the first course of action may expect pardon from God and man and may hope to improve their circumstances as Agathocles did. Those who follow the second course cannot possibly remain in power.

Therefore, it is to be noted that in seizing a state one ought to consider all the injuries he will be obliged to inflict and then proceed to inflict them all at once so as to avoid a frequent repetition of such acts. Thus he will be able to create a feeling of security among his subjects and, by benefiting them, win their approval. Anyone who acts otherwise, either through timidity or bad judgment, will always have to keep a dagger ready in his hand, nor will he ever be able to trust his subjects since, because of continually renewed injuries, they will never be able to feel safe with him. Injuries must be committed all at once so that, being savored less, they will arouse less resentment. Benefits, on the other hand, should be bestowed little by little so as to be more fully savored. Above all, a prince should treat his subjects in such a way that no event, whether good or bad, will cause him to alter his conduct. For punishments inflicted in time of dire necessity come too late to be useful; and the good that one does then will also be fruitless, for it will seem forced by circumstances, and no one will feel in any way grateful.

CHAPTER 9

CONCERNING THE CIVIL PRINCIPALITY

TURNING NOW to the other case, when a private citizen becomes the ruler of his country not through perfidy or intolerable violence but rather through the aid of his fellow citizens, we may call what ensues a civil principality (and neither exceptional ability nor unusual good fortune is needed to attain it, but only a certain fortunate cunning). I say that one becomes the ruler of such a principality through the support of either the common people or the nobles, for these two opposing parties are to be found in every city; and they originate from the fact that the common people do not want to be commanded or oppressed by the nobles, whereas the nobles do want to command and oppress them. From these conflicting desires will come one of three consequences: principality, liberty, or license.[1]

A principality, then, can come into being either by means of the common people or by means of the nobles, depending upon which of the two has the opportunity. When the nobles see that they can no longer withstand the people, they bestow power upon one of their own party and make him prince so that they can gratify their appetites under his protection. Likewise, when the common people see that they can no longer withstand the nobles, they bestow power upon someone of their own party and make him prince in order to find protection under his authority. The man who becomes prince through the help of the nobles will find it more difficult to remain in power than the man who becomes prince through the help of the people, for the former will be surrounded by men who will presume to be his equals. As a consequence, he will not be able to command them or control them as he would like.

But the prince who comes to power through the support of the people will stand alone, and there will be few or none at all near him who will not be disposed to obey him. Besides, it is impossible to satisfy the nobles fairly without injuring others, whereas it is indeed possible to do so with respect to the people, for their wishes have more right, since they seek to avoid oppression while the nobles seek to oppress. It should also be noted that a prince can never be secure against a hostile populace because it is numerous, whereas he can be secure against the nobles because they are few. The worst he can fear from a hostile people is to be abandoned by them, but from a hostile nobility he must fear not only being abandoned but also being attacked. Being possessed of more foresight and shrewdness, the nobles will not let slip any chance to protect their interests, and they will seek to gain favor with any potential winner. Moreover, a prince must of necessity accept the common people as he finds them, but he can very well do without any particular group of nobles, since he can make them and unmake them at any time by withdrawing or bestowing authority as he pleases.

Now to develop this point further, I say that nobles ought to be viewed in two principal ways: their procedure will be either to join their fortune to yours or to hold back from doing so. If they join theirs to yours and do not act rapaciously, you should honor and cherish them. But if they hold back, then again they must be viewed in two ways: they may do so through fear and natural lack of spirit, in which case you may make use of them, especially of those among them who are capable and judicious, for these nobles will bring you honor in prosperity and need not be feared in adversity. But when they avoid joining you, through cunning or ambition, that is a sign that they have more concern for themselves than for you. As regards these nobles, a prince must be on his guard, and he must fear them as though they were professed enemies, for in time of adversity they will be out to ruin him.

Thus one who becomes prince with the help of the people will have to preserve their good will—an easy matter, since they only ask that he avoid oppressing them. But one who becomes prince with the help of the nobles against the will of the people must above all else seek to win the good will of the people—again an easy matter so long as he will undertake to protect them. And since men become more obliged to their benefactor when they receive good where they had expected harm, the people will become more favorably disposed to the prince than they would have been if he had acquired power with their support. He can win their favor in many different ways; but since these vary according to circumstances, they cannot be reduced to rule. Therefore they will not be taken up.

I will conclude by saying only that the good will of the people is vital to a prince; otherwise he will be helpless in times of adversity. Nabis, prince of the Spartans, sustained attack from the whole of Greece and from a triumphant Roman army as well;[2] yet he was able to defend both his position and his country against them. To assure his safety when the danger arose, it was enough to take measures against only a few subjects; but if the populace had been hostile to him, such action would have proved inadequate. Now, let no one refute me with that trite proverb: "He who builds on the people builds on mud," for this is true only when a private citizen trusts in them and then deludes himself into thinking that they will rescue him if he is set upon by enemies or by the magistrates. In such a case he could often be mistaken, as was true for the Gracchi in Rome and for Messer Giorgio Scali in Florence.[3] But when the prince who trusts in them is a man of courage who is able to command, who is undismayed by adversity, who has not neglected his other defenses and can keep up the morale of his subjects by his orders and by his example, then such a man will never be deceived by them, and he will conclude that he has built his foundations well.

Usually a principality of this kind runs into difficulty when its civil structure is replaced by absolutism, for the prince of such a state rules either directly or through the magistrates. If the latter is the case, his position is all the weaker and the more dangerous, for then he is dependent upon those citizens who have been elevated to positions of authority and who can very easily deprive him of power, especially in time of trouble, either by opposing him or by not obeying him. Moreover, the prince will not have time to take power fully into his own hands when an emergency arises, because the citizens and subjects who have been used to taking orders from the magistrates in normal times will not be inclined to take orders from him in time of danger. Then, too, in moments of uncertainty there will always be a scarcity of men in whom to trust. The ruler of this form of state must not put faith in what applies in times of peace when the citizens need the government, for then everyone runs to him, everyone promises; all are ready to die for him when the risk of death is far off. But when trouble arises, when the government is in need of its citizens, few are found willing. This sort of experience is all the more dangerous because a ruler can have it only once. Therefore a wise prince must provide in such a way that, in whatever circumstances, the citizens will always be in need of him and of his government. Then they will always be loyal to him.

CHAPTER 10

How the Strength of All Principalities Should Be Measured

I N EXAMINING the character of these principalities, it is useful to take another matter into consideration, and that is whether the prince will have sufficient power and resources to stand on his own when the need arises, or whether he will always require the protection of others. By way of clarifying, I say that in my judgment the prince will be able to take care of himself if he has a sufficient supply of men or of money to put an adequate army in the field, capable of engaging anyone likely to attack him. It is also my judgment that he will always be dependent upon others for help if he is unable to meet his enemy in open battle and must take refuge behind his fortifications. As regards the first of these two possibilities, I have already spoken and will speak later on,[1] of what further is needed. As regards the second, there is nothing further to say, except to advise the prince who finds himself in this situation to provision and fortify his city and to have no concern for the surrounding countryside. Anyone who has provided carefully for the fortification of his city and has conducted himself toward his subjects as I have already indicated (and will further indicate later on) will never be attacked except with great reluctance. Men are always opposed to ventures in which they foresee difficulties, and it will not seem easy to attack a prince who has kept his city vigorously strong and is not hated by his people.

The cities of Germany enjoy great liberty. They possess but little territory beyond their walls; yet they obey the emperor only when they wish to,[2] fearing neither him nor any other of their powerful neighbors; for they are so well fortified that everyone is convinced it would be a wearying and difficult task to take them. They are all protected with suitable moats and walls and have adequate artillery. They always keep enough food, drink, and fuel in their public depots to last a year. Moreover, so that the common people may be fed without public expense, they have enough work of the sort that is the mainstay of the city to keep the populace engaged at their usual crafts for the space of a year. They also have a high regard for military exercises and have many regulations governing them.

Therefore, a prince in possession of a strong city who avoids arousing hatred is beyond danger of attack; and even if he should be attacked, his assailant would be forced to leave off in disgrace. For the affairs of the world are so changeable that it is impossible for an opponent to keep an army idle in the field for a year. Now, if someone were to interject that the people owning property outside the walls would lose patience when they saw it being set afire and that a long siege coupled with their own self-interest would cause them to forget their concern for the prince, I would reply that a bold and powerful prince could always overcome all such difficulties. He could at one time awaken his subjects' hopes that the trouble would soon be over, at another arouse their fear of the enemy's cruelty, at still another take skillful measures against the most outspoken of them. Besides, it is reasonable to assume that the enemy would pillage and burn the countryside immediately upon his arrival, at a time when the spirits of the defenders would still be hot and eager for their task. Thus the prince should have less to fear, for after a few days, when the spirits of his men will have cooled, the damage will already have been done, the injuries will have been received, and there will be no remedy. Then more than ever they will feel bound to their prince and will consider him under obligation to them, since their property will have been pillaged and burned in his defense. It is the nature of men to feel as much bound by the favors they do as by those they receive. Thus, if everything is properly considered, it will not appear difficult for a wise prince to keep up the determination of his citizens, both before and during a siege, so long as he does not lack food and the means of defense.

CHAPTER 11

CONCERNING ECCLESIASTICAL PRINCIPALITIES

ONLY ECCLESIASTICAL principalities now remain for us to discuss, and all problems concerning these are limited to the time preceding their acquisition. For though they are gained through ability or through fortune, they may be kept without one or the other because they are sustained by ancient laws rooted in religion that have proved capable of keeping princes in power no matter how they live or rule. Ecclesiastical princes alone can hold states without defending them, and subjects without governing them. Their states, though left undefended, are not taken from them, and their subjects, though left ungoverned, remain indifferent, lacking both will and strength to remove them. These states alone, therefore, are secure and happy.

And since they are sustained by superior causes which transcend human understanding, I will not discuss them. Because they are supported and exalted by God, it would be an act of presumption and rashness to speak of them. Still, if someone should ask how the Church attained such temporal greatness (despite the fact that up to the time of Alexander VI it was little respected among Italian rulers—not merely among the truly powerful ones but among all the petty lords and barons as well—while now she can make a French monarch tremble, drive him out of Italy, and ruin the Venetians), it may be useful to recall the major causes, though they are already well known.[1]

Before Charles VIII of France came into Italy,[2] this land was ruled by the Pope, the Venetians, the King of Naples, the Duke of Milan, and the Florentines. These powers had two principal objectives: the first was to see that no foreigner brought an army into Italy; the second was to see that none of these powers themselves took over more territory. The two of them that were held in deepest suspicion were the Pope and the Venetians. To keep the latter in check it was found necessary to form an alliance of all the others, as was done for the defense of Ferrara;[3] to keep the Pope in check it was found useful to rely on the barons of Rome. Since they were divided into two factions, the Orsini and the Colonna, these two baronial houses were forever finding cause for strife between them.[4] Always in arms under the pontiff's very nose, they had the effect of keeping him weak and inactive. And even though bold popes like Sixtus IV occasionally appeared on the scene,[5] they were either not fortunate or clever enough to free themselves of this obstacle. Moreover, the short span of a pope's reign—ten years on the average—made it difficult to suppress either of these factions. And if a pope did come near to crushing the Colonna faction, for example, another pope would succeed him who would restore it but have insufficient time to crush the Orsini. It is this situation that has caused the temporal power of the popes to be little respected in Italy.

Then came Alexander VI, who, of all the pontiffs there have ever been, was the first to show what a pope with money and troops could do. Using Duke Valentino as his instrument and the French invasion as his opportunity, he achieved all those things which I mentioned earlier in speaking of the Duke's enterprise.[6] Though his object had been to aggrandize the Duke rather than the Church, his achievements nevertheless did increase her power, since she fell heir to his labors following Alexander's death and the Duke's removal. Then came Julius II, who found the Church strong, in possession of all of Romagna, and free of those factious barons of Rome whom the strokes of Alexander had reduced to impotence. He also found the way still open to those methods of accumulating money which had never been employed until the time of Alexander.[7]

Julius not only pursued the same objectives as his predecessor but he extended them further. He sought to conquer Bologna, defeat the Venetians, and drive the French out of Italy; and he succeeded in all these enterprises, which are the more to his praise because he accomplished them all for the Church and not for private advantage.[8] He kept the Orsini and Colonna parties confined to the weak circumstances in which he found them; and though there might have been leaders among them quite capable of attempting a change, two things kept them in check: one was the power of the Church, which awed them; the other was that they had no cardinals among them to give rise to factional strife. These two parties will never be at peace when there are cardinals numbered among them, for it is they who nourish party conflicts both in Rome and elsewhere; and then the barons are compelled to engage in their defense. Thus it is that from the ambition of prelates, discords and broils are engendered among the barons. His Holiness Pope Leo has found the papacy very strong, and therefore it may be hoped that, as his predecessors made it great through the use of arms, he will make it revered and still greater through his goodness and his other countless virtues.[9]

CHAPTER 12

CONCERNING VARIOUS KINDS OF TROOPS, AND ESPECIALLY MERCENARIES

HAVING DISCUSSED in detail the various kinds of principalities which I mentioned in the beginning, and having to some degree considered the causes of their respective strengths and weaknesses and demonstrated the means by which many have sought to win and hold them, there now remains for me to discuss the means of offense and defense which these principalities can generally employ. I said earlier that a prince must build on sound foundations, otherwise his downfall is assured. The two most essential foundations for any state, whether it be old or new, or both old and new, are sound laws and sound military forces. Now, since the absence of sound laws assures the absence of sound military forces, while the presence of sound military forces indicates the presence of sound laws as well,[1] I shall forgo a consideration of laws and discuss military forces instead.

I say, therefore, that the troops with which a prince defends his state may be his own or they may be mercenaries or auxiliaries,[2] or a combination of these. Now, mercenary and auxiliary forces are useless and dangerous; and any ruler who keeps his state dependent upon mercenaries will never have real peace or security, for they are disorganized, undisciplined, ambitious, and faithless. Brave before their allies, they are cowards before the enemy. They show no fear of God, no faith toward men. A prince who employs them will stave off ruin only so long as he can stave off action. In peace he will be despoiled by them; in war he will be despoiled by his enemies. The reason for all this is that they have no tie of devotion, no motive for taking the field except their meager pay, and this is not enough to make them willing to die for him. They are quite anxious to be his soldiers so long as he avoids war, but let war come and they will either desert or flee.

I need hardly spend much effort to convince anyone of the truth of these observations, for Italy's ruin has had no other cause but the fact that for many years she relied upon mercenary forces. Some of these did indeed achieve a measure of success in a few instances and seemed very bold in fighting against each other. But as soon as foreigners invaded Italy, they showed what they really were. Thus King Charles of France was able to conquer Italy with a piece of chalk.[3] Whoever said that our sins were to blame for this spoke the truth.[4] It was not the sins he had in mind, however, but rather these I have mentioned; and since they were the sins of princes, princes have paid for them too.

I want to demonstrate the shortcomings of these troops more fully. Mercenary captains either are or are not skillful soldiers. If they are, you cannot trust them, for they will always seek to gain power for themselves either by oppressing you, their master, or by oppressing others against your wishes. If, on the other hand, they are not skillful soldiers, they will still be your ruin in most cases. Now, if someone should argue that any man in command of troops, whether mercenary or not, would do the same, I would answer that the control of troops should be in the hands of princes or republics. A prince ought to take personal charge and serve as commander; a republic ought to appoint one of its citizens. If the person appointed should prove incompetent, he ought to be replaced; if he should prove successful, there ought to be laws to keep him in bounds. Experience shows that only princes and republics with troops of their own have accomplished great things, while mercenary forces have brought nothing but harm. Moreover, a republic with troops of its own is less likely to be subjugated by one of its citizens than a republic using foreign troops.

Rome and Sparta remained armed and free for many centuries. Currently the Swiss are excellently armed and enjoy great freedom. Among the ancients the Carthaginians, for example, employed mercenaries and were nearly conquered by them after their first war with the Romans, even though these troops were commanded by citizens.[5] After the death of Epaminondas, the Thebans made Philip of Macedon their captain and, once victorious, he deprived them of their liberty.[6] After the death of Duke Filippo, the Milanese hired Francesco Sforza to fight the Venetians; yet once he had defeated them at Caravaggio he joined sides with them to subdue his own employers, the Milanese themselves.[7] After Francesco's own father had been hired by Queen Giovanna of Naples, he suddenly deserted her, leaving her without troops; whereupon she was compelled to fall into the clutches of the King of Aragon in order not to lose her kingdom.[8]

If the Venetians and Florentines did extend their territories in the past through the use of mercenaries whose commanders did not become their masters but defended them instead, then as far as the Florentines are concerned the reason is that they were lucky: for among the skilled captains whom they had cause to fear some proved unable to conquer, some had opposition, and some turned their ambitions elsewhere. One who could not conquer was Giovanni Aucut;[9] his loyalty, therefore, was never really ascertained, though everyone will admit that if he had been victorious the Florentines would have been in his power. The Sforzas were always opposed by the Bracceschi,[10] each eying the other suspiciously. Francesco Sforza finally directed his ambitions toward Lombardy, while Braccio directed his against the Church and the Kingdom of Naples. But let us turn to more recent events. The Florentines hired Paolo Vitelli—a very clever captain who had risen to a position of great importance from modest beginnings.[11] No one will deny that if this man had been able to defeat Pisa he would have had the Florentines at his mercy, for by defecting to their enemy he would have left them powerless, and so to keep him loyal they would have had to submit to him.

As for the Venetians, if we examine their operations we will note that they went forward securely and gloriously so long as they themselves fought their wars (and this was their policy until they turned their attentions to the mainland). With their own patricians and common people under arms they achieved great things. But as soon as they began to fight on land they gave up this advantage and adopted the methods of Italian warfare.[12] Owing to their great reputation and the modest size of their gains, they had little to fear from their captains during the first period of land conquests. But as soon as their territories increased, as they did under Carmagnuola, they got an early hint of their error. Having had proof of Carmagnuola's remarkable ability, by which they were victorious over the Duke of Milan, and having then noted his reluctance to go on with the war, they concluded that since he was no longer willing they could win no more under his command; still they could not dismiss him, lest they lose their gains thereby. And so for safety's sake they were compelled to execute him.[13] The Venetians then hired Bartolomeo da Bergamo, Ruberto da San Severino, the Count of Pitigliano, and the like to serve as captains. With these men they had to fear not gains but losses, as they later discovered at Vailà, where in one day Venice lost what it had taken her eight hundred years of painful effort to gain.[14] With mercenary troops gains are slow, belated, and weak, while losses are swift and crushing. Now, since my examples have brought me around to Italy, which has been controlled by mercenary troops for many years, I want to go more deeply into the subject so that once the origin and development of these forces have been understood, it will be easier to provide correction.

You must understand, then, that in recent years, while the

imperial power began to suffer defeats in Italy and papal authority began to increase in the temporal sphere, Italy became divided into many states. In many of the larger cities the people rose up against the nobles who, formerly supported by the emperor, had kept them in subjection.[15] The Church favored these revolts in order to gain temporal power. In many other cities one of the citizens became prince. Thus it came about that Italy was almost entirely in the hands of the Church and of some few republics. Since neither the clergy nor the citizens were acquainted with arms, they began to hire foreign troops. The first to make a reputation for these forces was Alberigo da Conio, of Romagna.[16] Braccio and Sforza, in their day arbiters of Italy, were, along with others, products of his training. After these came all the rest who have commanded troops of this kind in Italy down to our time. And the result of their prowess has been that Italy was overrun by Charles, plundered by Louis, ravished by Ferdinand, and dishonored by the Swiss.[17]

The aim of these captains was, first of all, to deprive the infantry of standing in order to enhance that of their own troops. This they did because, being entirely dependent upon their professional earnings for a livelihood (since they possessed no territories of their own), they found a large body of infantry impossible to feed and a small one insufficient to make a mark. Consequently they resorted to the use of cavalry, by which they could gain both a reputation and a livelihood. Things came to such a pass that in an army of twenty thousand troops there were not even two thousand foot soldiers. Moreover, these captains made every effort to eliminate hardship and danger for themselves and their soldiers. They did not kill each other in their assaults, but only took prisoners, even without expecting ransom. They did not attack towns by night, nor did those in the towns attack the enemy in their tents. They did not throw up stockades or dig ditches around their encampments, nor did they take to the field in winter. And all these things were permitted by their military code and, as before mentioned, had been invented by them in order to avoid hardship and danger, with the result that they have reduced Italy to slavery and shame.

CHAPTER 13

CONCERNING AUXILIARY, MIXED, AND NATIVE FORCES

A UXILIARY FORCES—the other kind of useless troops—are those supplied by a foreign power which has been called upon for assistance. Pope Julius II did this recently in his campaign against Ferrara when, noting the ineffectiveness of his mercenaries, he resorted to auxiliaries and arranged that Ferdinand of Spain should send his armies to help him.[1] Such forces may be useful and trustworthy in pursuit of their own interests, but they are almost always disastrous to the one who borrows them; for if they are defeated, he is ruined; and if they are victorious, he becomes their prisoner.

Even though ancient history is full of examples to prove this, I shall nevertheless stick to the fresh one provided by Pope Julius, whose action could hardly have been more ill-considered. In order to gain Ferrara, he put himself entirely at the mercy of foreigners. But his good fortune brought about a third complication which spared him the consequences of his unwise decision, for when his auxiliaries were routed at Ravenna, the Swiss arrived and, contrary to all expectations, including his own, they drove off the victors.[2] Thus he avoided becoming the prisoner of his enemies, who had fled, and likewise of his auxiliaries, since he had won with other arms than theirs. Being entirely unarmed themselves, the Florentines sent ten thousand French troops to subdue Pisa. As a result they experienced greater danger than ever they had in any other time of trouble.[3] To attack his neighbors, the Emperor of Constantinople sent ten thousand Turks into Greece. When the war ended, they refused to leave. This was the beginning of the enslavement of Greece by the infidels.[4]

Anyone wishing to be incapable of victory, therefore, may use troops of this kind, for they are more dangerous than mercenaries. With them ruin is assured. They are entirely united, entirely subject to another's orders. Mercenaries, on the other hand, need more time and better opportunity if they are to hurt you after they have gained a victory, since, having been assembled and hired by you, they are not united in one body. If you appoint a third party to be their leader, he cannot so quickly gain influence over them as to do you harm. In short, with mercenaries the danger lies in their cowardice; with auxiliaries, it lies in their capability.

Hence wise princes have always shunned such troops and have relied on their own; and they have thought it better to lose with their own troops than to win with those of others, judging it no true victory to win with another's arms, and I do not hesitate to cite Cesare Borgia and his actions for illustration.[5] This Duke entered Romagna with auxiliaries—all French troops— and with these he took Imola and Forlì. But then, judging them no longer reliable, he changed over to mercenaries, believing these to be less risky, and he hired Orsini and Vitelli. Finding these by turn hesitant, disloyal, and dangerous to manage, he did away with them and resorted to his own troops. One can easily see how much difference there is among the various kinds of troops by noting the difference in the Duke's reputation when he had French troops alone, when he had the Orsini and Vitelli, and when he was left with his own troops under his command. In each succeeding case it increased; nor was he ever highly esteemed until everyone saw that he was in complete possession of his own forces.

I had intended not to depart from recent Italian examples; still I do not want to overlook the case of Hiero of Syracuse, since I mentioned him earlier.[6] As I said, when the Syracusans made this man commander of the armies, he quickly perceived that their mercenary forces, being like our own hired Italian forces, were worthless. Judging that he could not safely keep them nor safely discharge them, he had them cut to pieces. Thereafter he made war with his own troops rather than with those of others. I should also like to call to mind a symbolic incident from the Old Testament which is relevant here. When David went before Saul and volunteered to go and fight Goliath, the Philistine champion, the King gave him his own sword and armor to encourage him. Having tried these on, however, David declined them, saying that he could not do well with them. Instead, he chose to face the enemy with his own sling and his own knife[7] In the end, the arms of another will fall from your hand, will weigh you down, or restrain you.

Charles VII, the father of Louis XI, having employed his fortune and his abilities to clear the English out of France, recognized the necessity of having his own arms and gave orders for the establishment of native cavalry and infantry units.[8] Later his son Louis abolished the infantry and began to hire Swiss mercenaries.[9] As we now can see, this mistake, repeated by others, is the cause of that kingdom's present peril. By enhancing the reputation of the Swiss, the King has demoralized his own forces; and by abolishing his infantry, he has made his cavalry dependent upon foreign arms. Having grown accustomed to fight with Swiss troops, the French now believe that they cannot win without them. Thus it happens that they are not up to opposing the Swiss and will not oppose others without them. French armies, therefore, are of mixed composition—part mercenary and part native. In combination, these are far superior to purely auxiliary or purely mercenary troops, but they are inferior to native ones. Let this example suffice, for the Kingdom of France would be invincible if Charles VII's orders had been maintained and extended. But men of little prudence will do a thing for immediate gain without recognizing the poison it bears for the future, as I indicated in my earlier reference to hectic fever.[10]

The man who does not recognize ills at their inception does not have true wisdom, and this is given to few. Anyone searching for the first cause of the ruin of the Roman Empire will find that it began with the hiring of mercenaries.[11] From that point the strength of the Roman Empire started to decline, and all the valor it lost was transferred to the Goths.

I conclude, therefore, that no state, unless it have its own arms, is secure. Indeed, it is a hostage to fortune, having no trustworthy power to defend it in adversity. It has always been the expressed opinion of wise men *"quod nihil sit tam infirmum aut instabile quam fama potentiae non sua vi nixae."*[12] By one's own forces I mean those composed of subjects, citizens, or dependents. All others are either mercenary or auxiliary. The way to organize one's own forces is easy to find if one examines the methods of the four individuals I have mentioned[13] and notes how Philip, the father of Alexander the Great, and many other rulers and republics raised and organized their troops. With their methods I am in full accord.

CHAPTER 14

A PRINCE'S CONCERN IN MILITARY MATTERS

A PRINCE must have no other objective, no other thought, nor take up any profession but that of war, its methods and its discipline, for that is the only art expected of a ruler. And it is of such great value that it not only keeps hereditary princes in power, but often raises men of lowly condition to that rank. It may be noted, on the other hand, that when princes have given more thought to fine living than to arms, they have lost their states. The first cause of losing them is the neglect of this art, just as the first means of gaining them is proficiency in it.

Through the pursuit of arms, Francesco Sforza rose from private citizen to become Duke of Milan; his sons, by shunning military hardships,[1] from dukes became private citizens, for among other ills which ensue from being disarmed is contempt, a disgrace which a prince must guard against, as I shall later explain. There can be no proper relation between one who is armed and one who is not; nor is it reasonable to expect that one who is armed will voluntarily obey one who is not, or that the latter will feel secure among servants who are armed. Since these will be inclined to show disdain and the prince to show suspicion, it is impossible that they should function well together. Consequently, a prince who is ignorant of military matters will find, along with the other ills mentioned, that he cannot have the esteem of his soldiers and cannot trust them.

Hence he must never turn his attention away from military exercises. Indeed, he should devote himself to them in time of peace even more than in time of war; and he may do this in two ways: through action and through study. As regards action, besides keeping his troops well disciplined and fit, he should devote himself to hunting, by means of which he may accustom his body to hardships and at the same time learn the topography of places—the slope of mountains, the opening out of valleys, the disposition of plains, the character of rivers and marshes— devoting much attention to these matters. Knowledge of this kind is useful to him in two ways. First of all, he becomes acquainted with the nature of his country and learns how it can be defended; secondly, by means of this acquaintance, he can the more readily understand the nature of any other place which he may subsequently have to reconnoiter. For the hills, valleys, plains, rivers, and marshes of Tuscany, for example, are in some respects like those in other provinces. Thus, from an understanding of the topography of one province he can easily acquire an understanding of others. The prince who lacks this ability lacks the first requirement of a commander, for by this he learns how to locate the enemy, how to choose quarters, how to advance upon the enemy, how to deploy his soldiers, and how to lay siege to cities with advantage.

Among other reasons why writers have praised Philopoemen, the leader of the Achaeans, is that in time of peace he thought of nothing but the manner of conducting war;[2] and when he was out in the country with friends he would stop and ask them: "If the enemy were on that hill and we had our army here, which would have the advantage? How could we advance on them in good order? If we wished to retreat, how would we go about it? If they were to retreat, how would we pursue them?" And as he went along he would set all the situations before them with which an army might be confronted. He would hear his friends' opinions, and he would give his own, supporting it with reasons. Thus, thanks to these continual deliberations, when he was at the head of his army no problem could ever arise for which he did not have the solution.

Now, as regards study, the prince ought to read history and

reflect upon the deeds of outstanding men, note how they conducted themselves in war, examine the causes of their victories and defeats, and thereby learn to emulate the former and avoid the latter. Above all, he ought to do as some wise men have done and take to imitating some celebrated predecessor whose deeds and actions he may keep ever before him—just as Alexander, it is said, imitated Achilles; Caesar imitated Alexander; and Scipio, Cyrus. Anyone who reads Xenophon's life of Cyrus will recognize how much of Scipio's glory derives from his imitating it and how closely he conformed to what Xenophon had written about Cyrus as regards continence, affability, humanity, and liberality. Every wise prince should pursue habits similar to these and never submit to idleness in time of peace, but rather endeavor to turn such time to advantage so as to profit from it in adversity. Thus, when fortune turns against him, he will be prepared to resist it.

CHAPTER 15

CONCERNING THINGS FOR WHICH MEN, AND PRINCES ESPECIALLY, ARE PRAISED OR CENSURED

IT NOW remains to consider what the attitude and conduct of a prince toward his subjects and friends should be. And since I know that many people have already written about these matters, I fear that I shall be considered presumptuous in writing about them, too, the more so because in treating this subject I depart from the rules set down by others. But since it is my intention to write something of use to those who will understand, I deem it best to stick to the practical truth of things rather than to fancies. Many men have imagined republics and principalities that never really existed at all. Yet the way men live is so far removed from the way they ought to live that anyone who abandons what is for what should be pursues his downfall rather than his preservation; for a man who strives after goodness in all his acts is sure to come to ruin, since there are so many men who are not good. Hence it is necessary that a prince who is interested in his survival learn to be other than good, making use of this capacity or refraining from it according to need.

Leaving fancies about princes aside, therefore, and considering only what is true, I say that when men (especially princes, who are most exposed to our view) are spoken of, they are marked for qualities which bring them either praise or censure. Thus some are called generous and others miserly (which is a Tuscan term, for in our language an avaricious person [*avaro*] is one who is avid for gain, while a miser [*misero*] is one who spares expense). Some are called openhanded, others rapacious; some cruel, others merciful; some untrustworthy, others faithful; some effeminate and weak, others fierce and bold; some courteous, others haughty; some lascivious, others chaste; some frank, others wily; some stubborn, others pliant; some grave, others merry; some religious, others unbelieving; and so forth. Everyone will admit that it would be very praiseworthy if a prince had all those above-named qualities that are deemed good; but since he cannot have them, nor devotedly adhere to them, because human conditions will not permit, he must be sufficiently prudent to avoid a reputation for those vices which would deprive him of his state and, if possible, also avoid those that would not deprive him of it. In case he is unable to avoid these last, however, he need not be overly concerned. Moreover, he need not be concerned if he acquires a reputation for those vices without which he would be unlikely to save his state. For, everything considered, he will find things which, though seeming good, will lead to his ruin if pursued, and others which, though seeming evil, will result in his safety and well-being.[1]

CHAPTER 16

CONCERNING LIBERALITY AND PARSIMONY

BEGINNING WITH the first of the above-named qualities then, I say that it would be well to be reputed generous. Yet to be so generous as to gain a reputation for this
quality is harmful. If one is prudently generous, as he ought to
be, the fact will not be noticed in him, nor will he escape censure for being miserly. To be reputed generous among men,
one must indulge in every form of ostentation, with the result
that any prince who does so will have to spend all of his resources and, to keep up his reputation, will have to burden his
people unduly by resorting to extortionate taxation and every
other means of raising funds. This will begin to make him odious to his subjects and, as he declines into poverty, will lose
him the respect of everyone. The outcome will be that, having
burdened the many and rewarded the few, he will feel the disadvantage of his position at the slightest sign of trouble and
will be exposed to danger. Once he recognizes his error, however, and seeks to amend it, he will quickly be labeled a miser.

Therefore, being unable to assume the virtue of liberality so
that it will be recognized and yet create no danger, a wise
prince will not object to being reputed a miser. With the passage of time he will come to seem more generous when it is
seen that, thanks to his parsimony, his income is sufficient to
his needs, that he can provide for his own defense against attack, and that he can undertake campaigns without burdening
his people. Thus he will demonstrate liberality toward all
those whom he does not tax—the many—and he will demonstrate miserliness toward all those from whom he withholds
largesse—the few.

In our day we have seen great things accomplished by none
except men who have been reputed parsimonious, the others
having been driven from power. After Pope Julius II had profited from a reputation for liberality to win the papacy, he made
no effort to keep it, so as to make war instead.[1] The present

King of France has engaged in so many wars without levying special taxes on his subjects because he has counterbalanced the extra expenses by his parsimony. The present King of Spain would never have undertaken and won so many campaigns if he had been reputed a generous man.[2]

Hence, if in his desire to avoid preying upon his subjects and provide for his defense, if to escape the contempt of poverty and shun rapacity, a prince should acquire a name for miserliness, he need not be concerned, for this is one of the vices which permit him to reign. Now, if someone were to say, "Caesar gained supreme power by being openhanded, and many others have attained high station by being so," I would answer: "Either a man is already a ruler or he is on the way to becoming one; if he is already a ruler, liberality will do him harm; if he is on the way, a reputation for liberality will indeed be necessary." Caesar was in process of attaining the Roman dictatorship; but if he had survived after attaining it and had not moderated his expenditures, he would have destroyed his authority. If someone were to reply, "There have been many princes who accomplished great things with their armies and yet were regarded lavishly generous," I would say: "A prince spends either his own and his subjects' funds, or he spends those of others. If the first is the case, he must be frugal; if the latter, he must neglect no part of liberality."

A prince at the head of an army who sustains himself by looting, pillaging, and extorting, handles property belonging to others and therefore must needs be generous; otherwise his troops would not follow him. What does not belong to him or to his subjects he may give away freely, as Cyrus, Caesar, and Alexander did, for by bestowing the goods of others he does not diminish, but rather increases, his standing. Only the expenditure of one's own resources is harmful; and, indeed, nothing feeds upon itself as liberality does. The more it is indulged, the fewer are the means to indulge it further. As a consequence, a prince becomes poor and contemptible or, to escape poverty, becomes rapacious and hateful. Of all the things he must guard against, hatred and contempt come first, and liberality leads to both. Therefore it is better to have a name for miserliness, which breeds disgrace without hatred, than, in pursuing a name for liberality, to resort to rapacity, which breeds both disgrace and hatred.

CHAPTER 17

CONCERNING CRUELTY: WHETHER IT IS BETTER TO BE LOVED THAN TO BE FEARED, OR THE REVERSE

TURNING TO some other of the aforementioned qualities, I say that every prince ought to wish to be considered kind rather than cruel. Nevertheless, he must take care to avoid misusing his kindness. Cesare Borgia was considered cruel; yet his cruelty restored Romagna, uniting it in peace and loyalty. If this result is considered good, then he must be judged much kinder than the Florentines who, to avoid being called cruel, allowed Pistoia to be destroyed.[1] A prince, therefore, must be indifferent to the charge of cruelty if he is to keep his subjects loyal and united. Having set an example once or twice, he may thereafter act far more mercifully than the princes who, through excessive kindness, allow disorders to arise from which murder and rapine ensue. Disorders harm the entire citizenry, while the executions ordered by a prince harm only a few individuals. Indeed, of all princes, the newly established one can least of all escape the charge of cruelty, for new states are encumbered with dangers. As Virgil has Dido say,

Res dura, et regni novitas me talia cogunt
Moliri, et late fines custode tueri.[2]

Nevertheless, he ought to be slow to believe what he hears and slow to act. Nor should he fear imaginary dangers, but proceed with moderation, prudence, and humanity, avoiding carelessness born of overconfidence and unbearable harshness born of excessive distrust.

Here a question arises: whether it is better to be loved than feared, or the reverse. The answer is, of course, that it would be best to be both loved and feared. But since the two rarely come together, anyone compelled to choose will find greater security in being feared than in being loved. For this can be said about the generality of men: that they are ungrateful, fickle, dissembling, anxious to flee danger, and covetous of gain. So long as you promote their advantage, they are all yours, as I said before, and will offer you their blood, their goods, their lives, and their children when the need for these is remote. When the need arises, however, they will turn against you. The prince who bases his security upon their word, lacking other provision, is doomed; for friendships that are gained by money, not by greatness and nobility of spirit, may well be earned, but cannot be kept; and in time of need, they will have fled your purse. Men are less concerned about offending someone they have cause to love than someone they have cause to fear. Love endures by a bond which men, being scoundrels, may break whenever it serves their advantage to do so; but fear is supported by the dread of pain, which is ever present.

Still a prince should make himself feared in such a way that, though he does not gain love, he escapes hatred; for being feared but not hated go readily together. Such a condition he may always attain if he will not touch the property of his citizens and subjects, nor their women. And if he finds it necessary to take someone's life, he should do so when there is suitable justification and manifest cause; but above all, he should refrain from the property of others, for men are quicker to forget the death of a father than the loss of a patrimony. Furthermore, excuses for seizing property are never lacking and, indeed, anyone who begins to live by plunder will always find pretexts for taking over what belongs to someone else. On the other hand, pretexts for taking someone's life arise more rarely and last a shorter time.

But when a prince is at the head of his armies and must

command multitudes of soldiers, then more than ever must he be indifferent to a reputation for cruelty, for without such a reputation no army was ever held together, nor was it ever fit for combat. Among the marvelous deeds of Hannibal is numbered this one: that though he had an enormous army composed of a great variety of races fighting in a foreign land, no dissension ever arose among the troops or between the troops and their leader, either in good times or in bad. This could have had no other source but his inhuman cruelty which, together with his extraordinary qualities of leadership, made him an object of constant reverence and terror to his soldiers. To produce such an effect without this cruelty, his other qualities would have been insufficient. Writers of scant judgment in this matter have, on the one hand, admired his accomplishments and, on the other, condemned their chief source.

The proof that his other qualities would have been insufficient may be seen in the case of Scipio—a most exceptional man not only in his own times but in all remembered history—whose soldiers mutinied in Spain for no reason other than his excessive leniency, which allowed them more freedom than was consonant with military discipline.[3] Fabius Maximus reproved him for it in the Senate and called him the corrupter of Roman arms.[4] When one of his lieutenants ravaged the Locrians, Scipio neither avenged them nor took action to correct his lieutenant's insolence. This too grew out of his mild nature, so much so, in fact, that someone seeking to excuse Scipio's conduct before the Senate observed that many men have more skill in avoiding errors than in correcting them. This propensity would in time have damaged Scipio's fame and glory if he had persevered in it, but since he was ruled by the Senate, its potential harmfulness remained hidden, and it redounded to his glory.

Returning to the question, then, of being loved or feared, I conclude that since men love as they themselves determine but fear as their ruler determines, a wise prince must rely upon what he and not others can control. He need only strive to avoid being hated, as I said.

CHAPTER 18

In What Way Princes Should Keep Their Word[1]

H OW PRAISEWORTHY it is that a prince keeps his word and governs by candor instead of craft, everyone knows. Yet the experience of our own time shows that those princes who had little regard for their word and had the craftiness to turn men's minds have accomplished great things and, in the end, have overcome those who governed their actions by their pledges.

You must recognize that there are two ways of fighting: by means of law, and by means of force. The first belongs properly to man, the second to animals; but since the first is often insufficient, it is necessary to resort to the second. Therefore, a prince must know how to use both what is proper to man and what is proper to beasts. The writers of antiquity taught rulers this lesson allegorically when they told how Achilles and many other ancient princes were sent to be nurtured by Chiron the centaur, so that he would train them in his discipline. Their having a creature half-man and half-beast as tutor only means that a prince must know how to use both the one and the other nature, and that the one without the other cannot endure.

Since a prince, then, is required to know how to assume a beastlike nature, he must adopt that of the fox and that of the lion; for a lion is defenseless against snares, and a fox is defenseless against wolves. Hence a prince ought to be a fox in recognizing snares and a lion in driving off wolves. Those who assume the bearing of the lion alone lack understanding. It follows, then, that a wise prince cannot and should not keep his pledge when it is against his interest to do so and when his reasons for making the pledge are no longer operative. If all men were good, this would be a bad precept, but since they are evil and would not keep a pledge to you, then you need not keep yours to them. Nor did a prince ever lack legitimate reasons by which to color his bad faith. One could cite a host of modern examples and list the many peace treaties, the many promises

that were made null and void by princes who broke faith, with
the advantage going to the one who best knew how to play the
fox. But one must know how to mask this nature skillfully and
be a great dissembler. Men are so simple and so much inclined
to obey immediate needs that a deceiver will never lack victims for his deceptions. Of recent examples proving this, there
is one I will not omit. Pope Alexander VI never gave thought
to anything but deception and never lacked someone on whom
to practice it.[2] There never was a man who made promises
more persuasively or swore to them more solemnly and kept so
few of them as he. Yet his tricks always brought the results he
desired, for he knew this side of the world well.

Therefore a prince will not actually need to have all the
qualities previously mentioned, but he must surely seem to
have them. Indeed, I would go so far as to say that having them
all and always conforming to them would be harmful, while
appearing to have them would be useful. That is, it will be well
for him to seem and, actually, to be merciful, faithful, humane,
frank, and religious. But he should preserve a disposition
which will make a reversal of conduct possible in case the need
arises. It must be understood, however, that a prince—especially
a prince who has but recently attained power—cannot observe
all of those virtues for which men are reputed good, because it
is often necessary to act against mercy, against faith, against
humanity, against frankness, against religion in order to preserve the state. Thus he must be disposed to change according
as the winds of fortune and the alterations of circumstance dic-
tate. As I have already said, he must stick to the good so long
as he can, but, being compelled by necessity, he must be ready
to take the way of evil.

Hence a prince must take care never to utter a word that is
not implicit with the five above-mentioned qualities; and he
must never appear to be anything but the very soul of
clemency, faithfulness, frankness, humanity, and religion to all
who see and hear him. But of all the qualities he must seem to
have, none is more important than the last. Generally, men
judge by the eye rather than the hand, for all men can see a
thing, but few come close enough to touch it. All men will see

what you seem to be; only a few will know what you are, and those few will not dare to oppose the many who have the majesty of the state on their side to defend them. In all men's acts, and in those of princes most especially, it is the result that renders the verdict when there is no court of appeal. Let the prince conquer a state, then, and preserve it; the methods employed will always be judged honorable, and everyone will praise them. For the mob is always impressed by appearances and by results; and the world is composed of the mob.[3] The few cannot prevail when the many have someone to rely upon. A certain ruler of our time, whom it is better not to name, preaches nothing but peace and faith, yet he is the extreme enemy of both; and if he had been true to either of them, he would more than once have lost either power or reputation.[4]

CHAPTER 19

HOW TO AVOID CONTEMPT AND HATRED

HAVING DISCUSSED the more important of the qualities previously mentioned, I would now like to discuss briefly the others under this general requirement: that the prince, as I mentioned earlier, endeavor to avoid those things which would make him the object of hatred and contempt. So long as he avoids these, he will have done his part and will encounter no risk at all from other vices. Hatred, as I said before, he will most readily engender by being rapacious and seizing the property and the women of his subjects. These he must not touch. The majority of men will be satisfied if he does not deprive them of their goods or their honor; and then he has only to contend with the ambitions of the few who may easily be restrained in many ways. He will engender contempt if he is fickle, frivolous, effeminate, cowardly, and irresolute. These characteristics he must guard against as ships guard against reefs; and he should conduct himself in such a way that greatness, boldness, gravity, and strength will be observed in his actions. In dealings with individual subjects, his decisions must be irrevocable; and he must maintain himself in such high regard that no one will ever think of cheating him or misleading him.

A prince who gives this sort of account of himself will be highly esteemed; and against someone who is highly esteemed, conspiracy is unlikely. Attack is also unlikely, so long as he is known to be respected by his subjects as an excellent man. For a prince has only two things to fear: one is internal and concerns his subjects; the other is external and concerns foreign powers. From the latter he protects himself with reliable troops and reliable allies—and he will always have reliable allies if he has reliable troops. Moreover, he will always enjoy quiet within his kingdom if there is quiet outside of it, unless it is disturbed by conspiracy. And even if foreign forces move against him, so long as he has things in order and has lived as I directed and, furthermore, keeps up his spirit, he will repel any attack, just as Nabis the Spartan did.[1]

As for his subjects, when there is no external attack, the prince must worry about hidden conspiracies, against which he will find security by avoiding hatred and contempt and by keeping the people satisfied. It is essential that he do this, as I have already explained at length. Indeed, the most potent remedy a prince can have against conspiracies lies in his not being hated by the populace, for those who conspire always believe that the death of the prince will please the people. When they suspect that their action will anger the people, they will not be so rash as to undertake it. The difficulties that conspirators face are very numerous; and experience shows that, though there have been many conspiracies, few have succeeded. A conspirator cannot act alone, yet he cannot seek for associates except among those who are disaffected. As soon as he has revealed his intentions to one of these, he has already provided that person with the means to remedy his dissatisfaction. Obviously, the recipient of a conspirator's confidence can hope for every advantage. In fact, seeing success assured on the one hand and seeing it encumbered with doubt and danger on the other, he must needs be either a very rare friend of the conspirator or a very obstinate enemy of the prince if he keeps his faith.

To put matters briefly, I say that on his side the conspirator has nothing but fear, jealousy, and the dread of pain, which demoralize him; while on his side the prince has the majesty of state, the law, his allies, and his government, which defend him. If the good will of the people is added to these advantages, it is impossible that anyone will be so rash as to conspire against him; for ordinarily a conspirator's fears endure only up to the perpetration of his evil intentions; but in this instance, with the people arrayed against him, he must fear the aftermath as well, and he cannot hope to find a safe refuge anywhere.

To support this, one could cite countless examples, but I will be content with one that happened within the memory of our fathers.[2] When Messer Annibale Bentivogli, grandfather of the present Annibale, was ruler in Bologna, the Canneschi clan formed a conspiracy and murdered him; and even though no members of his family survived except the infant Giovanni, the people rose up and slew all of the Canneschi. This was a consequence of the popularity the Bentivogli then enjoyed in Bologna. Their popularity was so great, in fact, that, with no member of the family left to rule in Bologna, the people sent to Florence where, according to report, there was an illegitimate offspring of the Bentivogli who had been brought up by a blacksmith. They summoned him back to Bologna and entrusted him with the rule until Giovanni reached his majority.

I conclude, then, that a prince need take little account of conspiracies if the people are disposed in his favor. If they are opposed and hate him, however, he must fear every incident and every individual. All well-ordered states and all wise princes have been diligent in seeking to avoid exasperating the nobles and in keeping the common people satisfied. For this is one of the most important duties that falls to a prince.

Among well-organized and well-governed kingdoms in our time there is France. It has a great many laws and governing bodies upon which the freedom and security of the king can rely. Of these, the first is the parliament and the authority entrusted to it.[3] For whoever planned the government of that kingdom recognized the ambition and insolence of the nobles and concluded that a bridle was needed to curb them. He also recognized the hatred of the nobles which fear had engendered among the common people, and he concluded that the latter needed reassurances. But he decided that neither of these duties should fall to the king, for if it did, the king would lose the favor of either one side or the other, according as he judged the controversies that arose between them. He decided instead that there should be a third tribunal which, without burdening the crown, should restrain the nobles and support the common people. There surely could have been no better, no more prudent arrangement than this, nor any greater source of security for the king. From it a noteworthy lesson may be drawn: princes should delegate unpopular duties to others while dispensing all favors directly themselves. I say again that a prince must respect the nobility, but avoid the hatred of the common people.

In reviewing the lives and deaths of certain Roman emperors, someone might suppose that their examples serve to disprove my opinion, seeing that some of them led thoroughly honorable lives, showed great courage, and yet lost the empire or were conspired against and murdered by their subjects. In answering such an objection, I should like to discuss the character of some of these emperors and demonstrate that the causes of their downfall do not conflict with what I have adduced. At the same time I shall set forth certain other considerations that ought to be noted by those who study the events of those times. For the purpose, it will suffice to take all the emperors from Marcus the Philosopher to Maximinus—that is, Marcus Aurelius, his son Commodus, Pertinax, Didius Julianus, Septimius Severus, his son Antoninus Caracalla, Macrinus, Elagabalus, Alexander Severus, and Maximinus.[4]

First, it should be noted that, whereas princes normally have only to contend with the ambition of the powerful and the insolence of the populace, the Roman emperors had a third problem to deal with: they had to contend with the cruelty and rapacity of their soldiers. This was so difficult a task that it proved the downfall of many. For it was hard to satisfy the soldiery and the people at the same time. The people loved peace and therefore loved moderate rulers; the soldiers loved rulers endowed with military spirit—insolent, cruel, and rapacious—who would employ these qualities against the people to gain them double wages and otherwise give vent to their own avarice and ferocity. The result of these circumstances was that those emperors whose experience or natural endowments had not earned them a great reputation by which to restrain both the soldiers and the people inevitably fell from power. The majority of them, especially those who were inexperienced with power, chose to please the soldiers and cared little about offending the people when they saw the difficulty of satisfying both sides. It was a necessary choice, for when princes cannot avoid being hated by one party or another, they must first seek to avoid the hatred of the general population. If they are unable to do this, however, then they must seek to avoid the hatred of that part of the population which is the stronger. Thus, those emperors who had but newly come to power, and were therefore in need of special support, turned to the soldiers rather than to the people. The result, whether they succeeded or failed, then depended upon their ability to keep the support of the soldiers.

For these reasons, of the three emperors, Marcus Aurelius, Pertinax, and Alexander Severus—all of whom lived moderately, loved justice, hated cruelty, behaved humanely and courteously—only Marcus escaped an unhappy end.[5] Only Marcus lived and died with honor because he came to the purple by right of succession and owed it neither to the soldiers nor to the people. Moreover, being endowed with many virtues that won him respect, he was able to keep both the people and the soldiers within bounds without ever arousing hatred or contempt. Pertinax, however, was made emperor against the wishes of the soldiers, who, having grown accustomed to licentious living under Commodus,[6] could not bear the sort of decent conduct to which he sought to restrict them. Thus having aroused hatred, to which contempt was added because of his old age, Pertinax fell at the very outset of his administration.

Here it is worth noting that hatred may be engendered by

good deeds as well as by bad ones. Therefore, as I said before, a prince who wishes to remain in power is often forced to be other than good. When the group whose support he deems vital to his survival is corrupt—be it the common people, the soldiers, or the nobility—he must follow their inclinations in order to satisfy them. In such a case, good deeds become his enemies.

But let us consider Alexander Severus, who was such a good man that among other praiseworthy acts attributed to him there is this one: in all fourteen years of his reign not a single person was executed without trial. Nonetheless, because he was reputed effeminate and submissive to his mother's rule, he fell into contempt, whereupon the army plotted against him and slew him.

If, on the other hand, we consider the characters of Commodus, Septimius Severus, Antoninus Caracalla, and Maximinus, we will find them all very cruel and rapacious. In order to please the soldiers they allowed them to commit every possible kind of outrage upon the people; and, except for Septimius Severus, all of them came to a bad end. Severus was such an able man that by keeping the good will of his soldiers he was able to reign with continued success, even though he oppressed the people.[7] His abilities aroused such wonder among both the soldiers and the people that, in a manner of speaking, the former remained respectful and satisfied while the latter were left astonished and amazed. Now, because this man's actions were especially outstanding and impressive for one who had newly come to power, I would like to point out briefly how well he could adopt the methods of the fox and the lion which, as I said earlier, a prince must needs imitate.

When Severus recognized the cowardliness of Emperor Didius Julianus,[8] he persuaded the army he was commanding in Slavonia that it should return to Rome and avenge the death of Pertinax, who had been murdered by the Praetorian guards. With this excuse to hide his own aspiration to the throne, he moved his army toward Rome, reaching Italy even before it was known that he had set out. Upon his arrival in Rome, the fearful Senate elected him Emperor and put Julianus to death. With this accomplished as a beginning, only two obstacles required removal before Severus could be master of the whole empire. One lay in Asia, where Pescennius Niger, who commanded the Asiatic legions, had had himself proclaimed Emperor;[9] the other lay in the West, where Albinus, who also aspired to the purple, was stationed.[10] Judging it dangerous to reveal himself as an enemy to both, Severus decided to attack Niger and to deceive Albinus. He wrote to the latter saying that since he had been elected emperor by the Senate, he wanted Albinus to be associated with him in that dignity. He presented him with the title of Caesar and, by consent of the Senate, made him his imperial partner. Albinus took these gestures to be sincere. But as soon as Severus had defeated and slain Niger and settled matters in the East, he returned to Rome, where he complained to the Senate that Albinus, scarcely grateful for honors received, had treacherously plotted to kill him. As a consequence Severus felt compelled to punish his partner's ingratitude. Then he marched off to attack Albinus in France, where he deprived him of his authority and his life.

Whoever examines this man's actions closely will find him to have been a very fierce lion and a most wily fox who was feared and respected by everyone and not hated by any of his troops. No one will marvel that he, but newly come to authority, was able to retain such great power; for his reputation protected him against the hatred which the people had conceived for him as a result of his rapacity. But his son Antoninus Caracalla was also endowed with some very excellent qualities which astonished the people and pleased the soldiers.[11] He was a soldier who could endure every hardship, a great despiser of every delicate food and every kind of softness. These qualities made the soldiers love him. Nevertheless, his cruelty was so fierce and boundless that by countless executions he substantially reduced Rome's population, and he massacred the whole of Alexandria's.[12] This made him odious to the entire world, and even those close to him began to tremble, with the result that he was slain by a centurion in the midst of his army.[13]

Here it is to be noted that princes are inescapably exposed to assassinations of the kind which are the work of desperate men. Anyone who has no fear of dying can harm them. Yet, since cases of this kind are very rare, princes have little cause to fear them. They need only avoid doing serious injury to their personal servants and to such of their aides as they keep near at hand. This was Caracalla's mistake, for he had shamefully consigned the centurion's brother to death and daily threatened the centurion himself with a similar fate, yet he still retained him as a bodyguard—an imprudent procedure that cost him his life.

But let us turn to Commodus who, as the son and heir of Marcus Aurelius, could very easily have remained in authority by the simple expedient of following in his father's footsteps.[14] This would have satisfied soldiers and common people alike. But, possessed of a cruel and bestial disposition, he chose instead to flatter the troops and encourage their licentiousness in order to plunder the people. On the other hand, with no regard for the dignity of his title, he often descended into the arena to engage in gladiatorial combats, and he indulged in other base pursuits as well which disgraced the imperial majesty and earned him the scorn of his soldiers. Then, after he had brought the hatred of the people and the contempt of the troops upon himself, a plot was hatched against him and he was murdered.

There remains to discuss the character of Maximinus, a very warlike man, elevated to the purple by his troops after the murder of Alexander Severus, whose softness had begun to annoy them.[15] Maximinus, however, did not wear it long because of two factors which made him hateful and contemptible. One had to do with his base beginnings as a Thracian shepherd—a fact everywhere well known which invited the general scorn. The other had to do with his extreme savagery, which became widely known through the cruelties committed by his prefects in the capital and elsewhere when he delayed journeying to Rome to take possession of the imperial seat. Thus the whole world was moved to disdain his base origins and to fear his ferocity, with the result that first Africa, then the Roman Senate and people, then all of Italy, and finally his own army, rebelled against him. Encountering difficulties in their siege of Aquileia, his troops grew angry at his cruelty and, having little to fear now that he had so many enemies, they slew him.

I would rather not discuss Elagabalus, or Macrinus, or Julianus, all three contemptible creatures who were soon put to death.[16] Instead, I shall bring the present discussion to an end by saying that princes of our day have less difficulty with this matter of making extraordinary concessions to their troops. Though they may be required to give it some attention, it is soon settled, because no present-day ruler keeps troops which are closely bound up with the government and administration of his provinces, as the armies of the Roman Empire were. Therefore, if it was more necessary in those days to satisfy the soldiers than the people, this was because the soldiers had more power than the people. Today, except in the case of the sultans of Turkey and Egypt, all rulers find it more necessary to satisfy the people than the soldiers, because the former now have more power than the latter.

I make an exception of the Turkish sultan, who always keeps twelve thousand infantry and fifteen thousand cavalry troops near at hand upon whom the security and strength of his kingdom depend. Above everything else, he must preserve their good will. The same applies to the sultan of Egypt, who, since his kingdom is entirely in the hands of his soldiers, must keep them favorably disposed, at whatever cost to the people. It is to be noted that the Egyptian sultanate differs from every other state and resembles the Christian papacy, which can be called neither hereditary nor new because the ruler's successor is not his son but someone elected to the position by persons authorized to make the selection.[17] Since this is an old-established procedure, the state cannot be called a new one, for none of the difficulties common to newly established states arise, and the long-standing laws of the state are set up to receive the new ruler as though he were its hereditary lord.

But returning to our proper subject, I say that anyone who considers the present discussion will see that either hatred or contempt brought about the downfall of the previously named emperors, and he will understand how it happened that though some chose one line of conduct and others chose its opposite, each line of conduct brought success to one and failure to the others. For it was fruitless and damaging that Pertinax and

Alexander Severus, being new rulers, chose to imitate Marcus Aurelius, who had come to the purple by right of succession. Likewise, it was ruinous for Caracalla, Commodus, and Maximinus to imitate Septimius Severus when they lacked the ability to follow in his footsteps. Indeed, a new ruler in a new state cannot imitate the actions of Marcus Aurelius, and he need not follow those of Septimius Severus. Instead, he should borrow from Septimius Severus those actions which are necessary to establish his authority and from Marcus Aurelius those that are useful and glorious in preserving a state that is already firmly established.

CHAPTER 20

WHETHER FORTRESSES AND MANY OTHER EXPEDIENTS THAT PRINCES COMMONLY EMPLOY ARE USEFUL OR NOT

IN ORDER to keep their lands secure, some princes have disarmed their subjects; others have prompted division within the cities they have subjugated. Some have nurtured animosities against themselves; others have sought to win the approval of those they initially distrusted. Some have erected fortresses; others have destroyed them. Now, although it is impossible to set down definite judgments on all of these measures without considering the particular circumstances of the states where they may be employed, I shall nevertheless discuss them in such broad terms as the subject itself will allow.

To begin with, there has never been a case of a new prince disarming his subjects. Indeed, whenever he found them disarmed, he proceeded to arm them. For by arming your subjects, you make their arms your own. Those among them who are suspicious become loyal, while those who are already loyal remain so, and from subjects they are transformed into partisans. Though you cannot arm them all, nonetheless you increase your safety among those you leave unarmed by extending privileges to those whom you arm. Your different treatment of the two categories will make the latter feel obligated to you, while the former will consider it proper that those who assume added duties and dangers should receive advantages. When you disarm your subjects, however, you offend them by showing that, either from cowardliness or from lack of faith, you distrust them; and either conclusion will induce them to hate you. Moreover, since it is impossible for you to remain unarmed, you would have to resort to mercenaries, whose limitations have already been discussed. Even if such troops were good, however, they could never be good enough to defend you from powerful enemies and doubtful subjects. Therefore, as I have said, a new prince in a newly acquired state has always taken measures to arm his subjects, and history is full of examples proving that this is so.

But when a prince takes possession of a new state which he annexes as an addition to his original domain, then he must disarm all the subjects of that new state except those who helped him to acquire it; and these, as time and occasion permit, he must seek to render soft and weak. He must arrange matters in such a way that the arms of the entire state will be in the hands of soldiers who are native to his original domain.

Our forefathers, especially those who were reputed wise, used to say that it was necessary to employ internal factionalism to keep possession of Pistoia and to employ fortresses to keep possession of Pisa.[1] For this reason they fomented party strife in some of their subject cities so as to hold on to them more easily. This policy may have been all right in those times, when in a sense Italy enjoyed a condition of balance among its various states.[2] But I do not believe it should be set down as a maxim for the present day, for I do not believe that factions ever do anyone good. In fact, it is inevitable that a city divided by faction will fall quickly to any approaching enemy. The weaker side within will always ally itself with the invader, and the stronger side will not be able to hold out alone.

Adopting the policy just described, Venice, as it appears, fostered Guelf and Ghibelline factions in her subject cities,[3] and though she never allowed them to come to bloodshed, she nevertheless encouraged enough dissension to keep the citizens quarreling among themselves and, therefore, unable to unite against her. As we can see, this did not turn out to her advantage, for when she was routed at Vailà,[4] one of these factions immediately rose up and deprived her of all her territories. Moreover, this policy argues weakness in the prince, for such divisions are never tolerated in a strong state. They are advantageous only in time of peace because they make it easy to control one's subjects. But when there is war, the inherent weakness of this policy becomes apparent.

Princes become great, doubtless, by overcoming opposition and by removing obstacles that are set in their way. Therefore, when fortune wants to bestow greatness on a new prince, who has more need of fame than hereditary princes do, she creates enemies and urges them on to attack him so that he may have cause to vanquish them; and thus he scales the heights with ladders they themselves provide for him. For this reason many believe that, when occasion serves, a wise prince will cunningly provoke opposition and then, by routing it, increase his own stature.

Princes, particularly those who are new, have found more loyalty and usefulness in men whom they held suspect at the inception of their rule than in men whom they initially trusted. Pandolfo Petrucci, the Lord of Siena, ruled his state more often with men whom he had suspected than with others.[5] But one cannot speak generally on this matter, because it varies according to the situation. I shall say only this: that men who are enemies at the beginning of a new regime and are the sort who need someone to lean on can always be won over by a prince without any difficulty. And they will be compelled to serve him with loyalty proportional to their need to cancel out with deeds the unfavorable opinion he had of them. Hence the prince will find them more useful than those who, enjoying his confidence, neglect their duties.

And since the subject demands it, I will not fail to remind any prince who has acquired a new state by the aid of its inhabitants that he soundly consider what induced them to assist him; if the reason is not natural affection for him, but rather dissatisfaction with the former government, he will find it extremely difficult to keep them friendly, for it will be impossible to please them. If he will carefully think the matter through in the light of examples drawn from ancient and modern affairs, he will understand why it is much easier to win the favor of those who were happy with their former government, and hence were his enemies, than to keep the favor of those who, out of dissatisfaction with the former rule, helped him to replace it.

In order to hold on to their domains with greater safety, princes have customarily erected fortresses to curb and restrain their enemies and to provide themselves with a refuge in the event of a sudden attack. Since this is a procedure that was employed of old, I praise it. Yet in our own time Messer Niccolò Vitelli is known to have dismantled two of the fortresses in Città di Castello in order to keep possession of that state.[6] When Guidobaldo, the Duke of Urbino, returned to his domain after having been driven from it by Cesare Borgia, he razed all its fortresses to their foundations, feeling that without them there would be less likelihood of his losing it a second time.[7] The Bentivogli took similar measures when they returned to Bologna.[8] Fortresses, then, are useful or useless according to the circumstances. If they prove helpful on the one hand, they prove harmful on the other. The matter may be considered as follows.

The prince who fears his subjects more than he fears foreign foes should erect fortresses; but the prince who fears foreign foes more than he fears his subjects should disregard them. The castle of Milan which Francesco Sforza built has caused and will still cause more trouble for the House of Sforza than any disorders in that state.[9] Not to be hated by his subjects is the best fortress a prince can have. If the people hate him, a fortress will not save him, for when the people take up arms against him they will never lack for foreigners to succor them. In our day, fortresses have not profited any ruler except the Countess of Forlì when her husband, Count Girolamo, was murdered. Thanks to her fortress, she was able to escape the assaults of the populace and wait until assistance arrived from Milan to recover her domains, for on that occasion circumstances were such that no foreigner could come to succor the people.[10] Later, however, when Cesare Borgia attacked her, and her subjects joined forces with him, the fortress was of little use to her. Then and previously it would have been better for her if she had not been hated by the people than to have had the fortress. Everything considered, therefore, I approve of those who erect fortresses and of those who do not. But I condemn anyone who, putting his trust in fortresses, will think it no great matter if he is hated by the people.

CHAPTER 21

WHAT A PRINCE MUST DO TO BE ESTEEMED

NOTHING WINS so much esteem for a prince as embarking on great enterprises and giving rare proofs of his ability. In our own times, for example, there is Ferdinand of Aragon, the present King of Spain, who may almost be called a new prince; setting out as a weak monarch, he proceeded to win so much renown and glory that he has now become the greatest king in Christendom. Anyone reviewing his undertakings will find all of them great, and some even extraordinary. At the start of his reign he attacked Granada, and that action served as the foundation of his power.[1] He began the campaign when he was free of other concerns and had no fear of being obstructed. He kept the barons of Castile so preoccupied with it that they could give no thought to rebellion. Meanwhile he gained standing and authority over them without their realizing it. With funds supplied by the Church and by the people, he was able to keep armies in the field and use that lengthy war as the foundation of his military power which has since brought him honor. Moreover, in order to embark

upon greater enterprises, always in the name of religion, he resorted to a pious cruelty, despoiling the Marranos and driving
them from his kingdom.[2] There could be nothing more pitiful
or unusual than this. Under the same cloak of piety he attacked
Africa; he undertook his Italian campaign; and lastly he has
made war on France.[3] Thus he has always planned and executed great things which have filled his subjects with wonder
and admiration and have kept them preoccupied. One action
has grown out of another with such rapidity that there has
never been time in which men could quietly plot against him.

A prince will also find it advantageous to resort to unusual
and distinctive acts in civic matters, like those that are reported
about Messer Bernabò of Milan,[4] and whenever someone does
something extraordinarily good or bad in civic life, he should
reward or punish him in a manner that will arouse considerable
comment. Above all, by every one of his actions a prince
should strive to win renown as a great man of excellent ability.

A prince also gains esteem when he acts as a true ally or true
enemy, that is, when he declares himself openly for or against
one of two conflicting parties—a policy that is always better
than neutrality. If two of your neighbors come to blows, it may
be that you will have reason to fear the victor, or it may be that
you will not. In any event, you will do well to declare yourself
and fight with determination. For if you do have reason to fear
the victor and do not declare yourself, you will surely become
his prey, to the satisfaction and joy of the losing party. Then
you will have no one to defend you and no one to offer you a
refuge. The victor will not want an uncertain ally who will not
be helpful in adversity, and the loser will not take you in because you were unwilling to risk your arms on his behalf.

When Antiochus invaded Greece to drive out the Romans at
the behest of the Aetolians, he sent envoys to the Achaeans, allies of the Romans, urging them to remain neutral. At the same
time the Romans urged them to take up arms on their behalf.
When the matter was brought to debate in the council of the
Achaeans and Antiochus' envoys argued for their neutrality,
the Roman envoy answered, "What they advise as the best policy, namely, that you avoid taking part in the war, is indeed

contrary to your own interests; without friendship, without honor, you will become the prize of the victor."[5]

It always turns out that the party that is not your ally calls for your neutrality, while your ally asks that you declare yourself by action. In order to avoid immediate peril, an irresolute prince most often embraces neutrality and most often comes to grief. When you boldly commit yourself and your ally wins, then even though he is powerful and you are left at his mercy, he will be under obligation to you, and there will be a bond of friendship between you. In such cases men are never so shameless, never so extraordinarily ungrateful as to oppress you. Moreover, victories are never so complete that the victor remains free of all restraints, especially as regards justice. On the other hand, if your ally loses, he will take you in and help you as best he can; and you will then become his partner in fortunes that may rise again.

When the two opponents are not so powerful that you may have reason to fear the victor, then it is even more expedient to take sides. Then you will be taking part in the ruin of one neighbor with the help of another who, if he were wise, would have fought to save him instead. If your ally wins—and with your assistance he cannot help but win—then he will be at your mercy.

Here it ought to be noted that a prince should avoid joining forces with someone more powerful than himself for the purpose of attacking another unless necessity compels him to do so, as I explained above; for by winning he then becomes the prisoner of his ally. As far as possible, a prince should avoid being left at the mercy of someone else. The Venetians joined France in attacking the Duke of Milan when they could have avoided it, and that was their downfall.[6] But when such an alliance cannot be avoided (as was the case with the Florentines when the Pope and Spain sent an army to attack Lombardy),[7] then a prince should take part for the reasons already discussed. And let no state suppose that it can choose sides with complete safety. Indeed, it had better recognize that it will always have to choose between risks, for that is the order of things. We never flee one peril without falling into another.

Prudence lies in knowing how to distinguish between degrees of danger and in choosing the least danger as the best.

A prince should also demonstrate that he loves talent by supporting men of ability and by honoring those who excel in each craft. Moreover, he ought to encourage his citizens peaceably to pursue their affairs, whether in trade, in agriculture, or in any other human activity, so that no one will hesitate to improve his possessions for fear that they will be taken from him, and no one will hesitate to open a new avenue of trade for fear of taxes. Instead, the prince ought to be ready to reward those who do these things and those who seek out ways of enriching their city or state. In addition to all this, at the appropriate time of year, he ought to keep the people occupied with festivals and spectacles; and since every city is divided into guilds or other corporate bodies, he ought to take these into account and assemble with them on occasions, thus giving proof of his affability and munificence, yet never failing to bear the dignity of his position in mind, for this must never be lacking.

CHAPTER 22

CONCERNING THE PRINCE'S MINISTERS

A MATTER of no small importance to a prince is the selection of ministers, for their competence or incompetence will depend upon his capacity to judge; and the first estimate of his intelligence will be based upon the character of the men he keeps about him. If they are capable and loyal, he will be reputed wise, for he will have demonstrated that he knows how to recognize their ability and keep them loyal to him. If they are otherwise, he will be judged unfavorably, for the first mistake a ruler can make lies in the selection of his ministers. No one who knew Antonio da Venafro, the minister of Pandolfo Petrucci, Lord of Siena, could have supposed the latter to be anything but a very able man, since he had chosen such a minister.[1]

Minds are of three kinds: one is capable of thinking for itself; another is able to understand the thinking of others; and a third can neither think for itself nor understand the thinking of others. The first is of the highest excellence, the second is excellent, and the third is worthless. It follows, then, that if Pandolfo's mind was not of the first kind, it was surely of the second. For when a prince can discern what is good and bad in the words and deeds of another, he will be able to distinguish between his minister's good and bad performance, praising the one and correcting the other, even though he lacks an inventive mind himself. Then the minister cannot hope to deceive him and will work reliably.

Now, as to the means by which a prince may learn the character of a minister, there is one that never fails. When you see a minister who thinks more about his own interests than about yours, who seeks his own advantage in everything he does, then you may be sure that such a man will never be a good minister, and you will never be able to trust him. For the man upon whom the charge of a state rests must never think of himself, but always of the prince, and he must never think of anything but what concerns the prince. On the other hand, in order to keep him loyal, the prince must think of his minister, honoring him, enriching him, placing him under obligation, sharing both distinctions and duties with him, so that his minister will recognize that he cannot do without the prince, so that his many honors and abundant wealth will prevent his desiring more, and his many responsibilities will cause him to fear a change of government. When the relations between ministers and princes stand thus, they may trust one another, and when they stand otherwise, the result will always be disastrous to both.

CHAPTER 23

How to Avoid Flatterers

O NE IMPORTANT point I do not want to overlook concerns a failing against which princes cannot easily protect themselves unless they are especially prudent or have good advisers. I refer to the flatterers with whom the courts of princes are crowded. Because men are so easily pleased with their own qualities and are so readily deceived in them, they have difficulty in guarding against these pests, and in attempting to guard against them, they run the risk of being scorned. For there is no way of avoiding flattery except by letting men know that they will not offend by telling the truth; yet if every man is free to tell you the truth, you will not receive due respect.

Therefore a prudent prince will pursue a third course, choosing the wise men of his state and granting only to them the freedom to tell him the truth, but only concerning those matters about which he asks, and no others. Yet he should question them about all matters, listen to their opinions, and then decide for himself as he wishes. He should treat these councils and the individual advisers in such a way as to make it clear that their words will be the more welcome the more freely they are spoken. Except for these men, he should listen to no one, but rather pursue the course agreed upon and do so resolutely. Anyone who does otherwise will fall victim to flatterers or, as a result of the various opinions he hears, will often change his mind and thereby lose reputation.

Regarding this, I should like to cite a recent example. Pre' Luca,[1] the ambassador of Maximilian, the present emperor, used to say that His Majesty never sought counsel from anyone, yet never did anything as he wished to do it. This grows out of his acting contrary to what has just been suggested. Being a very secretive man, the Emperor never consults anyone and never reveals his intentions. But as soon as he begins to put them into effect, they are discovered. Then they are opposed by the men he has about him, and, lacking resolution, he is easily dissuaded from them. The result is that what he does on one day he destroys on the next, and it is never possible to know what he is seeking or planning, or to have any confidence in his decisions.

A prince, therefore, should always seek advice, but only when he, not someone else, chooses. Indeed, he should discourage everyone from giving advice unless he has asked for it. In fact, if he should observe that someone is withholding the truth for some reason, he should show annoyance. Since many people believe that some princes are reputed wise, thanks rather to their wise counselors than to their own natural gifts, they ought to be told that they deceive themselves. For this is a general rule that never fails: a prince who is not wise himself cannot be wisely counseled, unless by chance he should have a sole counselor by whom he is ruled in all matters. There could be such a situation, but it would not last long, for the counselor would soon deprive the prince of his state. An unwise prince, having to consider the advice of several counselors, would never receive concordant opinions, and he would not be able to reconcile them on his own. His counselors would pursue their own interests and he would know neither how to rule them nor how to understand them. They could not do otherwise, for men will always prove bad unless necessity compels them to be good. Therefore I conclude that good advice, no matter where it comes from, ultimately derives from the prudence of the prince, and the prudence of the prince does not derive from good advice.

CHAPTER 24

WHY THE PRINCES OF ITALY HAVE LOST THEIR STATES

WISELY PURSUED, the advice I have given above will make a new prince appear to have been long established in his state, and it will bind him more securely and more firmly to it than if he had actually been long established there. The actions of a new prince are more closely watched than those of a hereditary prince, and when they are recognized to be fitting and able, they win men over and compel their allegiance more than ancient lineage does; for men are more taken with the present than with the past. When they find themselves well off in the present, they enjoy it and seek nothing more. Indeed, so long as the prince does not neglect his duties, they will undertake to defend him in every way. Thus he will win a double glory for having initiated a new rule and for having endowed and strengthened it with sound laws, sound arms, and sound examples—just as he who, having been born a prince and having lost his dominion through imprudence, wins a double disgrace.

If we consider those rulers in Italy who have lost their dominions in our time—the King of Naples, the Duke of Milan,[1] and others, we will first of all find a common defect in them regarding arms, as I have already explained at length,[2] then we will find that they either alienated their people or, having kept them favorably disposed, failed to secure themselves against the nobility. Without these defects, states that have the strength to put an army in the field are not lost. Philip the Macedonian—not the father of Alexander, but the one who was defeated by Titus Quintius—ruled a state that was weak in contrast to the Roman and Greek powers that attacked him. Yet because he was a soldier who knew how to satisfy the people and secure himself against the nobles, he was able to endure many years of warfare against them. And if in the end he lost possession of some cities, he nonetheless kept possession of his kingdom.[3]

Therefore these princes of ours who were long in possession of their states must not blame fortune but rather their own sluggishness for having lost them. Because throughout the years of peace they had never considered that the times might change (for it is a common failing of men not to take account of tempests during fair weather), when adversity struck they thought of flight instead of defense, and they hoped that the people, irritated by the insolence of the victors, would summon them to return. This is a good refuge when all others are lacking, but it is foolish to abandon other expedients for it. No one should ever allow himself to fall down in the belief that someone else will lift him to his feet, because it will not happen; or if it does happen, it will not prove to his advantage. Such a means of defense is cowardly, in that it does not derive from one's own initiative, and only those methods of defense which depend upon one's own resourcefulness are good, certain, and enduring.

CHAPTER 25

CONCERNING THE INFLUENCE OF FORTUNE IN HUMAN AFFAIRS, AND THE MANNER IN WHICH IT IS TO BE RESISTED

I AM not unaware that many men have believed and still believe that the affairs of the world are controlled by fortune and by God in such a way that the prudence of men cannot manage them, and indeed cannot improve them at all. For this reason they are inclined to think that there is no point in sweating much over these matters and that they should submit to chance instead. As a consequence of the great changes, exceeding every human expectation, that have been and are still seen daily, this opinion has had wider acceptance in our day than heretofore. Thinking about it, I myself have sometimes been inclined to concur with this judgment in some measure.

Nevertheless, since our free will must not be denied, I estimate that even if fortune is the arbiter of half our actions, she still allows us to control the other half, or thereabouts. I compare fortune to one of those torrential rivers which, when enraged, inundates the lowlands, tears down trees and buildings, and washes out the land on one bank to deposit it on the other. Everyone flees before it; everyone yields to its assaults without being able to offer it any resistance. Even though it behaves this way, however, it does not mean that men cannot make provision during periods of calm by erecting levees and dikes to channel the rising waters when they come, or at least restrain their fury and reduce the danger.

The same may be said about fortune, which tends to show her strength where no resources are employed to check her. She turns her course toward those points where she knows there are no levees or dikes to restrain her. Now, if we consider Italy, the scene and the agent of the changes I have referred to, we will observe that she is a land without bulwarks or any other defenses, for if she were guarded by suitable forces, as Germany, France, and Spain are, then these inundations would not have produced such enormous changes, or they would not have occurred at all. Let it suffice to have said this much about opposition to fortune in general.

But limiting myself to particulars, I would like to point out why it is that we see a prince safely in power on one day and overthrown on the next, though there has been no change in his character or behavior. This derives first of all, I think, from those causes which I explained at length some time back—that is, from the fact that a prince who relies entirely upon fortune will fail when his fortune changes. It also derives, I think, from the fact that a prince is successful when he fits his mode of proceeding to the times, and is unsuccessful when his mode of proceeding is no longer in tune with them. We note that men pursue the ends they have in view, that is, glory and wealth, by different ways. One uses caution while another is impetuous, one resorts to violence while another relies on craft, one acts patiently while another does the contrary; and each reaches his goal by a different route. We also note that of two men who employ caution one will gain his objective while the other will not, or that both will gain their objectives by different means, one by being cautious, the other by being impetuous. The cause of this is nothing other than the character of the times to which these modes of conduct may or may not be suited. It is this, as I have said, that explains how two men using different methods will achieve the same results, and two others using similar methods will achieve contrary results—the one succeeding, the other failing.

This also explains the inconstancy of prosperity. If one is

cautious and patient in his method of proceeding and the times
lend themselves to this kind of policy, he will prosper. But if the
times and circumstances change, he will fail, for he will not alter
his policy. There is no man so prudent that he can accommodate
himself to these changes, because no one can go contrary to the
way nature has inclined him, and because, having always pros-
pered in pursuing a particular method, he will not be persuaded
to depart from it. Hence, when the times require it, the cautious
man will not know how to act impetuously and he will be overthrown. If he were able to adapt his nature to changing times and
circumstances, however, his fortunes would not change.

Pope Julius II acted impetuously in everything he undertook, and he found the times and circumstances so well suited
to this way of acting that he always met with success. Consider
his first campaign against Bologna when Messer Giovanni
Bentivogli was still living.[1] The Venetians did not like it; neither did Spain. Negotiations were still going on about it with
France. Nevertheless, with characteristic fierceness and haste
he set the campaign in motion, leading it in person. This suddenness reduced the Venetians and Spain to inaction, the one
because of fear and the other because it hoped to recover the
lost territories of the Kingdom of Naples. It also had the effect
of involving the King of France who, being desirous of the
Pope's help in defeating the Venetians, concluded that he
could not deny him troops without manifestly injuring him.

Thus, by his impetuous action, Pope Julius achieved what
no other pontiff would have achieved by all possible prudence.
If he had delayed his departure from Rome until everything
had been settled and arranged, as another pontiff would have
done, he would never have succeeded, because the King of
France would have made a thousand excuses and the others a
thousand threats to thwart the enterprise. I will not speak of his
other ventures, for they were all alike and all of them succeeded well. His short life spared him any contrary experi-
ences. If the time had come when caution would have been
required, it would have brought his downfall, for he would
never have abandoned those methods to which his own nature
inclined him.

Therefore, since fortune changes while human beings remain constant in their methods of conduct, I conclude that men will succeed so long as method and fortune are in harmony and they will fail when these are no longer in harmony. But I surely think that it is better to be impetuous than to be cautious, for fortune is a woman and in order to be mastered she must be jogged and beaten. And it may be noted that she submits more readily to boldness than to cold calculation. Therefore, like a woman, she always favors young men because they are not so much inclined to caution as to aggressiveness and daring in mastering her.

CHAPTER 26

AN EXHORTATION TO FREE ITALY FROM THE HANDS OF THE BARBARIANS

HAVING DULY pondered everything so far discussed and having asked myself whether the present circumstances of Italy were auspicious for honoring a new prince and whether conditions were potentially suited for a prudent and resourceful man to shape them so as to win honor for himself and well-being for her people, I have concluded that so many things favor a new prince that I can think of no more fitting time for this purpose. And, as I said before, if the Israelites had to be in Egyptian bondage before Moses could demonstrate his resourcefulness, if the Persians had to be oppressed by the Medes before Cyrus could make manifest his greatness of spirit, if the Athenians had to be scattered before Theseus could display his excellence[1]—then, before the resourcefulness of an Italian spirit could be made known in the present, Italy had to be reduced to her present state, more enslaved than the Hebrews, more servile than the Persians, more scattered than the Athenians, leaderless, disordered, beaten, despoiled, bruised, trampled, subjected to every kind of injury.

And although there may have been someone before now who aroused some glimmer of hope that he had been ordained by God for her redemption, still we afterward saw how fortune rejected him at the critical point of his enterprise.[2] Thus, left almost lifeless, Italy awaits the arrival of someone who may heal her wounds, put an end to the sacking of Lombardy, to the exactions of tribute from the Kingdom of Naples and from Tuscany and cure her long-festering sores. See how she prays God to send her someone who will rescue her from barbarian insolence and cruelty. See, too, how ready and anxious she is to rally to any banner, so long as there is someone to raise it aloft.

Nor is it possible to see where she may look more hopefully at present than to ycur illustrious house which, with its fortunes and merits favored by God and by the Church it now rules, can provide the leadership for her redemption.[3] The task will not be difficult if you will keep before you the lives and deeds of those I have just named. And although they were rare and extraordinary men, yet they were men, and each had less opportunity than the present occasion affords. Their task was neither more just nor easier than this one, nor did God favor them more than he favors you. There is great justice in this cause, *"iustum enim est bellum quibus necessarium, et pia arma ubi nulla nisi in armis spes est."* [4] There is great readiness here, and where there is great readiness, there can be no great difficulty, so long as your house will seek to emulate those whom I have proposed as models. Moreover, unparalleled wonders have been seen, wrought by God. The sea has parted, a cloud has shown the way, a stone has poured forth water, manna has rained down from the sky;[5] all things have conspired to show your greatness. The rest you must do yourself. God is unwilling to do everything Himself lest He deprive us of our free will and of that portion of glory that belongs to us.

And there is no reason to marvel if the Italians previously referred to failed to achieve what may be hoped for from your

house, or if, in so many revolutions and in so many exploits of
arms, Italian military prowess has repeatedly appeared to have
become extinct. This derives from the fact that the old ordinances are no good and there has been no one capable of establishing new ones. Nothing so much honors a man newly come
to power as the new laws and new ordinances he brings into
being. Such things, when they are well based and impressive in
scope, win reverence and admiration; and in Italy there is no
lack of matter awaiting the impress of new forms. The individual members here show great qualities when the same are not
lacking in their leaders. Consider duels and combats involving
few men and note how superior Italians are in strength, in nim-
bleness, and in skill. But when it comes to armies they do not
show up well. This stems from the weakness of their leaders.
The competent ones are not obeyed, and everyone thinks he is
competent because no one up to now has been able to stand out
so clearly above the other leaders in skill and fortune that they
would yield to him. The result has been that over a long span
of time, in the many wars that have been fought in the past
twenty years, every all-Italian army involved in them has made
a bad showing. The first proof of this came at the Taro, then at
Alessandria, Capua, Genoa, Vailà, Bologna, and Mestre.[6]

Therefore, if your illustrious house wishes to emulate the
great men who have redeemed their countries, you must above
all provide yourself with troops of your own as the true foundation of every undertaking; for there cannot be more loyal,
truer, or better soldiers than these. If each of them is individually effective, they will be even more effective as a unit when
they see themselves commanded by their own prince, who favors and honors them. Hence it is necessary to plan to have
such troops so that Italian valor will be able to defend us from
the foreigner.

Though the Swiss and Spanish infantry are considered very
formidable, each has a weakness that would enable a third kind
of infantry not only to oppose them but confidently to overcome them. The Spanish cannot sustain cavalry attacks, while
the Swiss are fearful of any as determined as their own. Thus it
has been observed, and experience will prove it, that the Spanish

infantry cannot withstand a French cavalry attack, and the Swiss infantry can be routed by the Spanish. Though experience has not actually shown this last assertion to be true, nevertheless there was a hint of it at the Battle of Ravenna, where the Spanish infantry confronted the German battalions, which are the same kind as the Swiss.[7] There the Spaniards, aided by their agility and their bucklers, broke in under the long pikes of the Germans and attacked them with impunity, leaving them with no recourse. And if the cavalry had not dislodged them, the Spaniards would have slain them all. Having recognized the defects of both these orders of infantry, one can devise a new kind which will withstand cavalry forces and not be afraid of other infantry. This can be accomplished by the creation of new weapons and by changes in military formations. It is things of this kind which, newly introduced, bestow fame and greatness on a new prince.

This opportunity, therefore, must not be allowed to pass, so that Italy after so long a time may find her redeemer. I cannot describe with how much love, with what thirst for revenge, with what resolute loyalty, with what tenderness, with what tears he would be received in all those provinces which have endured these foreign hordes. What gates would be closed to him? What people would deny him obedience? Whose envy would oppose him? What Italian would withhold his allegiance? This barbarian domination stinks in everyone's nostrils. Let your illustrious house take up this task, then, with that boldness and with that hope which is reserved to just enterprises, so that this nation may be ennobled under your banner and so that under your auspices the words Petrarch wrote may come true:

Against barbarian rage,
Virtue will take the field; then short the fight;
True to their lineage,
Italian hearts will prove their Roman might.[8]

Discourses Upon the
First Ten Books of
Titus Livy

BOOK ONE

2. Of the Various Kinds of States and of What Kind the Roman Republic Was

I WANT to leave aside any discussion of cities which from their outset were subject to foreigners, and I shall speak instead of those which came into being entirely free of external domination and governed themselves as they chose, either as republics or principalities, by diverse laws and ordinances according to their diverse origins. For some, either at their founding or shortly after, were given laws all at one time, as Lycurgus gave them to the Spartans,[1] while others acquired theirs by chance at different times as the result of particular events. Happy is that state which produces a man prudent enough to provide it with laws and institutions by which it may live securely without any need to alter them. We note that Sparta observed her laws for eight hundred years without corrupting them and without experiencing any dangerous disorders. Less happy, to a degree, is that state which, having found no prudent lawgiver, has been compelled to devise its own laws. Still less happy is the one which is further removed from civic order; and least happy of all is the one whose institutions are entirely off the path that leads to a right and perfect end. For states in this last case, it is scarcely possible that their institutions will be set right by some event or other. Those that are not perfectly ordered but have made a proper beginning conducive to improvement may by circumstance become perfect. But this is surely true: they will never be reorganized without running into danger, for the majority of men will not accept new laws designed to introduce new institutions in the state unless they are shown the necessity for them. Since such a necessity cannot arise except in event of danger, it is likely that the state will perish before it is ever brought to a perfect order. Ample proof of this is the republic of Florence, which was reorganized in 1502 as a result of events in Arezzo and was overthrown in 1512 as a result of events in Prato.[2]

In wishing to discuss Rome's form of government and the events that led to its perfection, I must observe that some who have written about states have asserted that these take three forms—monarchical, aristocratic, and democratic—and that those who organize the government of a state must turn to the one of these which seems most suitable. Still other writers, whom many consider even wiser, assert that there are six kinds of government, of which three are bad and three others, though good in themselves, are so easily corrupted that they too must be deemed pernicious. The good ones are the three forms mentioned above. Each of the three bad ones are parallel to one of them, and each so closely resembles its like that the leap from the one to the other is easy; for monarchy easily becomes tyranny, aristocracy easily becomes oligarchy, and democracy easily converts to anarchy. Thus anyone organizing a government according to one of the good forms does so for but a short time, because no precaution will prevent it from slipping into its opposite, so closely are the virtues and vices of the two related.

These various kinds of government came into existence among men by chance, for in the beginning of the world, the inhabitants being few, they lived dispersed for a time in the manner of beasts. Then, as the population increased, they drew together and, the better to defend themselves, they sought out the strongest and bravest one among them, made him their leader, and obeyed him. From this beginning came a recognition of what is proper and good, as opposed to what is pernicious and wicked. Seeing a benefactor injured, men came to feel hatred and sympathy. They censured the ungrateful and praised those who showed gratitude. Realizing that similar injuries could be done to them, they decided to make laws to prevent this and to ordain punishments for those who violated them. From this came the recognition of justice. Thereafter, when it came time to elect a ruler, men no longer sought the boldest man among them but the most prudent and just instead.

But when, later on, rulers came to power by succession instead of by election, the inheritors of power soon degenerated and, abandoning the pursuit of worthy deeds, they came to feel that the prince had nothing to do except exceed all others in sumptuous living, lascivious behavior, and every other kind of license. Thus it happened that the prince began to be hated, began to fear; and thus passing quickly from fear to overt injury, he soon became a tyrant. This was the beginning of disorders, conspiracies, and plots against princes, initiated not by weak and timid men, but by those who, exceeding all others in generosity, magnanimity, wealth, and nobility, could not endure their prince's dishonorable conduct. Under the leadership of these powerful men, the masses took up arms and, having removed the prince, gave their allegiance to them as their liberators. Despising the very name of a single chief, these men constituted themselves a government; and at the beginning, mindful of the tyranny that had just been ended, they ruled in accordance with the laws they instituted, subordinating every personal advantage to the common good, governing and protecting both private and public matters with utmost care. When the administration passed to their sons, who had never known the vicissitudes of fortune or experienced wrongs and had become weary of civic equality, they gave way to greed, to ambition, to seizing women; and thus they transformed the government from an aristocracy into an oligarchy which had no regard for any civic right. Consequently, within a short time they suffered the same fate as the tyrant. Exasperated with their government, the masses were at the disposal of anyone designing in any way to attack their rulers; and soon someone came forward who with their help put an end to them. Having just destroyed a government of the few and having no desire to restore the rule of a prince—the memory of their former prince and of his offenses still being fresh in their minds—the masses had recourse to a democratic form of government. This they organized in such a way that neither the few nor a single prince would have any authority in it. And since all governments enjoy some respect at their outset, this democratic government survived for a time, but not for long, especially after the generation which had established it passed on. For anarchy, respectful of neither private citizens nor public men, soon followed, with the result that, each person acting as he pleased, every day saw a thousand wrongs committed. Thus, either through necessity or through the suggestion of some good man or through the desire to bring anarchy to an end, they returned to the rule of a prince. From here they moved step by step toward anarchy again, in the manner and for the reasons just described.

This is the cycle through which the governments of all states pass and have passed. Rarely, however, do they actually return to the same forms, for scarcely any state has the vitality to undergo many of these mutations and still survive. What will often happen is that at some moment of crisis, lacking both counsel and strength, the state will be subjugated by some neighboring one which enjoys better rule. If such did not occur, a state would be capable of passing through these various forms of government an infinite number of times.

I say, therefore, that all these kinds of government are harmful in consequence of the short life of the three good ones and the viciousness of the three bad ones. Having noted these failings, prudent lawgivers rejected each of these forms individually and chose instead to combine them into one that would be firmer and more stable than any, since each form would serve as a check upon the others in a state having monarchy, aristocracy, and democracy at one and the same time.

Among those who have merited praise for employing such a constitutional form is Lycurgus, who, by setting up the laws of Sparta in such a way as to provide a place for king, aristocracy, and people, created a state which lasted more than eight hundred years, bringing great credit to him and peace to his city. In establishing the laws of Athens, Solon did the contrary, for by organizing a popular government, he created one which was so short-lived that even before his death it gave way to tyranny under Pisistratus.[3] Though the latter's heirs were driven out forty years later and Athens returned to liberty, because it again adopted the popular form Solon had given it, it did not last more than a hundred years, despite the many changes of constitution designed to repress the arrogance of the rich and the license of the multitude, which Solon had not foreseen. Despite all this, by comparison with Sparta's, the government of Athens endured but a short time because Solon had failed to provide a place in it for monarchical and aristocratic power.

But let us turn to Rome. Though it lacked a Lycurgus at its outset to organize it in such a way that it could long enjoy freedom, in consequence of disagreements between the plebs and the Senate it experienced so many internal vicissitudes that chance provided what a legislator had failed to provide. If Rome was not among the very most fortunate states, it was surely among the second most fortunate. If her first institutions were defective, still they did not deviate so far from the right direction that they could not be brought to perfection. Both Romulus and the other kings established many good laws compatible with a condition of freedom. But since their aim had been to found a kingdom and not a republic, when the city obtained its freedom it still lacked many things necessary for the furtherance of freedom, which the kings had failed to establish. And though the kings lost their sovereignty for the reasons previously discussed, nevertheless those who drove them from power by quickly appointing two consuls to serve in place of the king, in effect drove only the name of king and not the royal power out of Rome. Thus, having the consuls and the Senate, the state came to combine two of the three aforementioned forms of government, that is, monarchy and aristocracy. Only popular government lacked a place. And when the Roman nobility became insolent, for reasons I shall explain below, the people rose up against them, so that in order that all should not be lost, it was found necessary to assign them their part, while the Senate and the consuls retained enough power to preserve their position in the state. Thus the Tribunes of the plebs were created, and the state attained greater stability because all three forms of government now had a share in it.[4] And fortune proved so favorable that, though the government did pass by stages from king to aristocrats to the people for reasons I have already given, nevertheless monarchical power never passed entirely into the hands of the aristocrats, nor did aristocratic power ever pass completely into the hands of the people. Retaining its mixed composition, the state thus reached perfection—a perfection it owed to the dissension between the plebs and the Senate, as the following two chapters will show.

3. The Events That Led to the Creation of the Tribunes of the Plebs, by Which the Roman Republic Became More Perfect

A S ALL those who write about civic matters show and as all history proves by a multitude of examples, whoever organizes a state and establishes its laws must assume that all men are wicked and will act wickedly whenever they have the chance to do so. He must also assume that whenever their wickedness remains hidden for a time there is a hidden reason for it which remains unknown for want of occasion to make it manifest. But time, which is called the father of all truth, uncovers it.

After the Tarquins had been expelled from Rome,[1] it seemed that the plebs and the Senate enjoyed a most harmonious relationship, that the nobles had put away their characteristic haughtiness and had become imbued with the spirit of the common people so that even the lowest wretch found them tolerable. This deception remained hidden for so long as the Tarquins survived; for the nobles, fearing the Tarquins and fearing that the plebs, if ill-treated, would seek to make common cause with them, behaved decently toward the common people. But no sooner had the Tarquins died and thus removed their cause of fear, than the nobles began to spit out all the venomous hatred of the plebs which they had kept pent up in their bosoms, and they injured them in every way they could. This is proof of what I said above, namely, that men will never do good except by necessity. Whenever they have the freedom to choose and the chance to act with abandon, they introduce confusion and chaos everywhere. That is why it is said that poverty and hunger make men industrious and that laws make men good. Whenever things go well of themselves there is no need for law; but as soon as good habit fails, the law must be quickly invoked. Thus, with the passing of the Tarquins, fear of whom had kept the nobles in check, it became necessary to introduce a new order which would produce the same conditions that had obtained while they were still living. Consequently, after many disorders, alarms, and threats of violence between the plebs and the nobles, the Tribunes were instituted to provide for the security of the plebs. These were invested with so many prerogatives and so much authority that they could always function as mediators between the plebs and the Senate and put down the insolence of the nobles.

4. THAT THE DISORDERS BETWEEN THE PLEBS AND THE SENATE MADE THE ROMAN REPUBLIC STRONG AND FREE

I DO not want to neglect considering the disorders that occurred in Rome in the period between the death of the Tarquins and the establishment of the Tribunes, nor mentioning several things in opposition to the common belief that Rome was a disorderly republic, full of so much dissension that if fortune and military prowess had not counterbalanced these defects it would have been the inferior of all other republics. I cannot deny that fortune and military prowess were the sources of Roman power. But what the critics I have referred to fail to see is that wherever there are sound military forces there must also be sound institutions, and rarely does it happen that there is not good fortune as well. But let us turn to other particulars regarding that city.

It seems to me that those who condemn the conflicts between the plebs and the nobles are condemning the primary source of Rome's liberty and are giving more consideration to the tumult and the shouting these conflicts aroused than to the good effects they produced. They fail to observe that there are two different factions in every republic—the common people and the aristocrats—and that all laws enacted to increase liberty derive from the conflict between them, as we can easily see from what happened in Rome. From the Tarquins to the Gracchi[1]—a period of more than three hundred years—the disorders in Rome rarely brought banishment and still more rarely brought bloodshed. On such slight grounds it is impossible to call these disorders harmful, or to call a republic divided if in so long a span of years her discords resulted in the banishment of no more than eight or ten citizens and in the execution of a scant few. Not too many were even sentenced to pay fines. Nor can a republic reasonably be deemed disorganized where there are so many examples of virtue, for good examples derive from sound training, sound training from sound laws; and in this case the sound laws derived from the conflicts that many men have unwisely condemned. Anyone properly examining the consequences of these conflicts will find that they produced no banishments or acts of violence detrimental to the common welfare, but they did produce laws and institutions that promoted public liberty. Now, someone might say that such proceedings were unusual and almost inhuman—to see the people assemble and cry out against the Senate, the Senate cry out against the people, to see the people storm through the streets, shops shut down, all the plebs march out of Rome—things frightening even to read about. I say that all cities must have devices by which the people can demonstrate their concern and interest, especially those cities which intend to engage the people in important undertakings. Among other devices Rome had these: when the people wanted a law enacted they behaved as I have described or they refused to enlist for the wars. Consequently, in order to placate them it was necessary to satisfy their wishes in some way; and the wishes of free people are seldom damaging to freedom, for they grow out of oppression or the fear of being oppressed. When these fears are unjustified, there is recourse in the public assemblies where some reputable man can rise and speak to them and show them they are wrong. The people, as Cicero says, may be ignorant, but they can recognize the truth and will readily yield when some trustworthy man explains it to them.

The Roman government, therefore, ought to be censured more sparingly, and it ought to be recognized that all the good things that came out of that republic could have had none but the soundest of causes. If these discords caused the establishment of the Tribunes, they deserve utmost praise; for besides giving the people a share in the government, the Tribunes served as the guardians of Roman liberty as will be shown in the next chapter [omitted here].

10. FOUNDERS OF REPUBLICS AND KINGDOMS ARE AS MUCH TO BE PRAISED AS FOUNDERS OF TYRANNIES ARE TO BE CENSURED

AMONG PRAISEWORTHY men, the most praiseworthy are leaders and founders of religions; after them come founders of republics and kingdoms; next most to be praised are those who, as commanders of armies, have extended the boundaries of their kingdom or country. To these we add men of letters and, since these are of various kinds, they are honored according to their rank. To all other men, who are infinite in number, we assign some measure of praise in the degree that they merit it through their occupation or craft. Infamous and detestable, on the other hand, are the destroyers of religion, the wreckers of kingdoms and republics, the enemies of virtue, of learning, and of every other art that benefits and honors the human race. Such are the irreligious, the violent, the ignorant, the useless, the slothful, the cowardly. There will never be anyone so ignorant or so wise, so bad or so good who, being asked to choose between the one kind of men and the other, will not praise the praiseworthy and censure the blameworthy. Nonetheless, nearly all men, deceived by a seeming good or a seeming glory, willingly or unknowingly slip into the ranks of those who are more deserving of blame than of praise; and being able to establish a kingdom or a republic that would win them everlasting honor, they establish a tyranny instead. They do not realize how much fame, how much glory, how much honor, security, tranquillity, and satisfaction of mind they lose by this choice, and how much infamy, shame, censure, danger, and affliction they incur.

If they would read history and profit from the records of the past, it is impossible that the private citizens of a republic would not rather be Scipios than Caesars, or that anyone who through fortune or ability becomes a ruler would not rather be an Agesilaus, a Timoleon, or a Dion than a Nabis, a Phalaris, or a Dionysius,[1] for they would see the latter roundly condemned and the former highly applauded. They would also see that Timoleon and those like him had no less authority in their native lands than Dionysius and Phalaris had in theirs, and enjoyed far more security.

Now, let no one be deceived by Caesar's glory when they see him so much praised by the historians, for those who praise him were corrupted by his good fortune and were awed by the long duration of the Empire, which, continuing to rule under his name, did not permit writers to speak openly about him. But anyone who wishes to know what they would have said about him if they had been free may judge by what they wrote about Catiline;[2] and in proportion as the one who commits an evil is more to be censured than the one who merely plans to commit it, just so is Caesar the more blameworthy of the two. One may also judge by the praise they heaped upon Brutus; being unable to condemn Caesar because of his power, they turned to praise his enemy instead.

Let anyone who has become the ruler of a republic also consider how much more praise, after Rome had become an empire, was merited by those emperors who lived by its laws, like good princes, than by those who lived in the contrary fashion. He will observe that Titus, Nerva, Trajan, Hadrian, Antoninus, and Marcus Aurelius did not need Praetorian guards or masses of troops to protect them, because their own good behavior, the good will of the people, and the love of the Senate protected them. He will also see that the Western and

Eastern armies were not enough to save Caligula, Nero, Vitellius, and many other wretched emperors from the enemies which their evil habits and their wicked lives had aroused. If the history of these men were well considered, it would provide many lessons for a ruler and point out to him the ways of glory and of shame, of security and of fear. Of twenty-six emperors from Caesar to Maximinus, sixteen were assassinated and ten died naturally. If among those who were assassinated some good ones like Galba and Pertinax are to be numbered, their deaths must be attributed to the corruption which their predecessors had introduced among the soldiers; and if among those who died naturally some bad ones like Severus are to be numbered, this must be attributed to their unusual good fortune and ability—characteristics that few men combine. From these lessons of history a ruler may also learn how a good kingdom can be established, for he will observe that of the emperors who came to power by inheritance all except Titus were bad, that of those who came to power by adoption—like the five from Nerva to Marcus Aurelius—all were good, and that when the Empire fell to heirs, it resumed the path to ruin.

Therefore, let a prince consider the period from Nerva to Marcus Aurelius and compare it with the one preceding it and the one following it. Then let him choose in which of these he would have preferred to live or in which he would have preferred to rule. In the period ruled by good emperors, he will see the ruler secure among secure citizens in a world of peace and justice. He will see a Senate enjoying its authority, magistrates enjoying their honors, wealthy citizens enjoying their wealth; he will see nobility and virtue exalted, tranquillity and well-being everywhere, with all rancors, all license, corruption, and ambition extinguished. He will see a golden age in which every man can hold and defend any opinion he likes. Finally, he will see the world in triumph: the prince revered and exalted, the people loving and secure. If he will then duly examine the times of the other emperors, he will see them wracked by savage wars, torn by seditions, by cruelty in peace and war alike; he will see many princes perish by the sword, many civil and foreign wars; he will see Italy afflicted by a host of misfortunes, her cities sacked and ruined, Rome in ashes, her capitol destroyed by her own citizens, her temples desolate, her rites corrupted, her cities rampant with adulteries, her seas filled with exiles, her shores flooded with blood; he will see innumerable cruelties committed in Rome, with nobility, wealth, acquired honors, and, above all, virtue treated as capital offenses; he will see slanderers rewarded, servants turned against their lords, freedmen against their masters, and those lacking enemies oppressed by their friends. Then he will recognize the debt that Rome, Italy, and the world owes to Caesar.

Then, surely, if he is born of woman, he will be shocked at the thought of imitating and reviving those wretched times, and he will be kindled with an immense desire to emulate the good ones. Indeed, a prince seeking for glory in the world should be glad to possess a corrupt city, not to ruin it completely, as Caesar did, but to reform it, as Romulus did. Indeed, the heavens can offer men no greater opportunity for glory, nor can men desire a greater. Now, if a prince wishing to reform a city were thereby obliged to abdicate and refused to do so out of a desire to retain his rank, he would have some excuse. But if he were able to reform it and keep his rank, he would have no excuse at all. In short, let those to whom the heavens grant such an opportunity realize that two ways lie before them: one of them assures them of security while living and of glory after death; the other assures them of continual troubles while living and of eternal infamy after death.

11. On the Religion of the Romans

THOUGH ROME had its first founder in Romulus, to whom, as a daughter, she owed her birth and training, nevertheless the heavens, judging that his institutions would prove insufficient for so great an empire, inspired the Senate to elect Numa Pompilius as his successor so that Numa could attend to whatever Romulus had left undone. Finding a savage people and wishing to reduce them to civil obedience through the arts of peace, Numa turned to religion as a necessary instrument for the maintenance of a civil society, and he constituted it in such a way that for many centuries there was nowhere so much fear of God as in that republic. This facilitated whatever enterprise the Senate or the great Roman leaders wished to embark upon. Anyone who reviews the innumerable deeds of the Roman people collectively and those of many individual Romans will observe how the citizens stood in far greater fear of breaking an oath than of breaking a law, as though they had more regard for God's might than for man's. This is manifestly demonstrated in the actions of Scipio and of Manlius Torquatus. After Hannibal had routed the Roman armies at Cannae, many citizens assembled together and, fearing for their country, agreed to forsake Italy and go to Sicily. Hearing of this, Scipio went to them and, sword in hand, made them swear that they would not abandon their country. Lucius Manlius, father of that Titus Manlius afterward called Torquatus, was indicted by Marcus Pomponius, the Tribune of the people. Before the case came to trial, Titus went to Marcus and, threatening to kill him if he did not swear to withdraw the indictments against his father, induced him to swear to do so; and so greatly did Marcus respect an oath that he withdrew the indictment. Thus those citizens who could not be kept in Italy either by love of country or by its laws were kept there by an oath they were forced to take; and thus a Tribune overlooked his hatred for a father, the injury of a son, and the claims of his own honor to obey his sworn oath. All this had no other origin but the religion which Numa had introduced into the city.

Let those who study Roman history duly note how useful religion was in directing the armies, in animating the people, in keeping men good, and in shaming the wicked. Thus, if we were to dispute whether Rome owed a greater obligation to Romulus or to Numa, I think the latter would take first place; for where there is religion, it is easy to introduce military discipline, but where there is military discipline and no religion, the latter can only be introduced with difficulty. And it may be observed that

Romulus did not need the authority of God to establish the Senate and other civil and military institutions, but it was indeed necessary for Numa, who pretended to have conversations with a nymph from whom he received the counsels he passed on to the people. This he did because he wanted to introduce new and unaccustomed laws into the city and doubted that his own authority would prove sufficient.

And in fact there was never anyone who ordained new and unusual laws among a people without having recourse to God, for they would not otherwise have been accepted. This is so because prudent men know of many beneficial things which, having no persuasive evidence for them, they cannot get others to accept. Consequently, wise men who wish to avoid this difficulty resort to divine authority. Lycurgus, Solon, and many others who had the same objectives in view did this. Marveling at Numa's wisdom and goodness, the Roman people therefore yielded to all his proposals. It is true, however, that because those were very religious times and because the people with whom he had to deal were ignorant, he was greatly facilitated in executing his designs and in impressing every new form upon them. Doubtless anyone wishing to set up a republic at the present time would find it easier to do so among mountaineers, where civilization is lacking, than among those who are accustomed to the cities, where civilization is corrupt. A sculptor will more easily extract a beautiful statue from a piece of rough marble than from one that has been badly blocked out by someone else.

Everything considered, then, I conclude that the religion which Numa introduced into Rome was one of the primary causes of her prosperity, for that was the source of good laws; good laws bring good fortune, and from her good fortune ensued all the happy results of her enterprises. As the observance of religious rites is the foundation of a republic's greatness, so disrespect for them is the source of its ruin. Where a fear of God is lacking, the state must either fail or be sustained by a fear of the ruler which may substitute for the lack of religion. But since rulers live only a short while, such a state must vanish as soon as the abilities that sustained it have vanished. Hence it follows that states which rest solely upon a man's abilities are of short duration and pass from the scene when his abilities are no more; and it seldom happens that they are renewed in his successor. As Dante wisely says:

> Seldom does human probity ascend
> From branch to branch; and this He wills, who gives it,
> That being sought from Him, it may descend.[1]

Therefore, the welfare of a republic or kingdom does not lie in its having a prince who governs it prudently while he lives, but rather in having one who organizes it in such a way that it may endure after his death. And though it is easier to persuade rude men to accept a new order or new opinions, this does not mean that it is impossible to do the same with cultivated men and with those who think they are not rude. The people of Florence do not think they are ignorant or rude, yet Girolamo Savonarola convinced them that he conversed with God.[2] I would rather withhold judgment as to whether this was true or not, for one must speak respectfully of so great a man. But I will certainly say that multitudes believed him without ever having seen anything extraordinary to compel their believing it. His manner of life, his teachings, and the matters he dealt with were enough to win their confidence. No one should therefore fear that he cannot accomplish what others have accomplished, for, as I said in the preface, men are born, live, and die in quite the same way as they always have.

12. THE IMPORTANCE WITH WHICH RELIGION MUST BE REGARDED AND HOW ITALY, LACKING IT, THANKS TO THE CHURCH OF ROME, HAS BEEN RUINED

P RINCES AND republics concerned with keeping the state from corruption must above all see to it that their religious ceremonies remain uncorrupted and continue to be properly

venerated, for every religion has its vital source in some one of
its principal institutions. Pagan religious life was based upon
the responses of the oracles and upon the order of soothsayers
and diviners. All the other ceremonies, sacrifices, and rites depended upon these, for the people quite readily believed that the
God who could predict their future good or future evil could
also bestow it. From this derived the temples, the sacrifices, the
supplications, and all the other rites of veneration. Hence the
oracles of Delos, the temple of Jupiter Ammon, and other celebrated oracles that filled the world with wonder and devotion.
When later the words of the oracles began to reflect the will of
the men in power and the people recognized the deception, they
lost faith and became capable of disrupting all good civic order.

The rulers of republics or kingdoms must therefore seek to
preserve the principles of their religion. Having done this, they
will find it an easy matter to keep the state devout, obedient,
and united. They should seek to favor and strengthen every circumstance that tends to enhance religion, even if they themselves judge it to be false. The wiser they are about natural
reality, the more they should do this. Because wise men ad-
hered to this rule, faith in miracles took root even among the
false religions, for these wise ones sought to promote them,
whatever their source, and lent them their authority so that they
came to be believed by everyone. Of this sort of miracles there
were many in Rome. Among others, there was this one that
took place while the Roman soldiers were sacking the city of
the Veii:[1] A number of them entered the temple of Juno and,
having approached her image, they said to it: "Do you wish to
come to Rome?" Some of them thought she nodded; others
thought that she said, "Yes." Because the soldiers were very
religious (as Titus Livy shows, for they had entered the temple
without making noise, devoutly and reverently), they became
convinced that they had heard the answer they had in a way expected. Camillus and the other chiefs of the city entirely favored this opinion and belief and elaborated it.

If the rulers of Christian lands had kept religion true to the
principles set down by its founder, the states and republics of
Christendom would be more united and happier than they are.

But there is no better evidence of its decline than to see how the people who are closest to the Church of Rome, the center of our religion, have the least faith. Anyone examining the principles of our religion and observing how far present practice has strayed from them would doubtless conclude that ruin or severe punishment is at hand.

Because many believe that the well-being of the Italian cities derives from the Church of Rome, I would like to present such arguments as occur to me in opposition to this view, and I will propose two very potent ones which, in my judgment, cannot be refuted. The first is that, because of the bad examples set by the court of Rome, this land has lost all reverence and religion, with the result that a host of troubles and disorders have followed; for just as we may suppose every advantage to accompany religion, so may we suppose the contrary to be the case where it is lacking. Our first debt to the Church and her priests is that, thanks to them, we Italians have become irreligious and wicked. But we owe it a still greater debt—the second cause of our ruin: that is, that the Church has kept and still keeps this country divided. Surely no country was ever happy or unified until it was all under the rule of a single republic or a single prince, as is the case with France and Spain. And the reason that Italy is not in the same situation and is not ruled by a single republic or a single prince is the Church alone. Though located in Italy and holding temporal power in it, she has had neither the strength nor the ability to subjugate the Italian tyrants and become the ruler; on the other hand, when threatened with the loss of her temporal dominions, she has not been so weak as to be unable to bring in some foreign power to defend her from any Italian lord who had become too strong. We know this well from long experience, as when by means of Charlemagne she drove out the Longobards who had become the rulers of nearly all of Italy, or when in our own day she deprived the Venetians of power through the aid of France. Later she drove the French out through the aid of the Swiss.[2] Thus, having lacked the strength to conquer Italy, and having refused to let others conquer her, the Church has seen to it that the country could not be dominated by a single ruler but has had many princes and lords instead. The result has been that she has become so weak and disunited as to become the prey not merely of powerful barbarians but of anyone attacking her. We Italians owe this to the Church, and to no one else. Anyone desiring positive proof of this so as to see the truth more clearly should have the power of relocating the court of Rome, with all the authority it now enjoys in Italy, in the territories of the Swiss who, as regards religion and military discipline, are the only people who live as the ancients did. Then in a short while he would see the wicked habits of that court creating more disorder in those lands than any other event could ever give rise to at any time.

58. THE MULTITUDE IS WISER AND MORE CONSTANT THAN A PRINCE

NOTHING IS more useless and more inconstant than the multitude. So says our author Titus Livy, and so also do all other historians affirm. For in the records of human actions we often find instances of a man's being condemned to death by the multitude and then being bitterly mourned and wished alive again by the same multitude, as the Roman people did in the case of Manlius Capitolinus, whom they condemned and then longed to have back again.[1] Of this incident our author says, "In short, when he no longer constituted a danger, the people were overcome with regret." Elsewhere, when he relates the events which took place in Syracuse after the death of Hieronymus, grandson of Hiero, he says, "Such is the nature of the multitude—either humbly to submit or haughtily to dominate."[2]

Now, I do not know whether I take upon myself a task so hard and so full of difficulties that I shall have to abandon it, or whether I shall be able to carry it through with perseverance, since my object is to uphold a view that, as I have said, all writers have opposed. Whatever the case, I do not believe and never shall believe it wrong to defend any opinion with reason, without recourse to authority or force.

I say, then, that this defect with which writers charge the multitude may also be charged to individual men, and particularly to princes, for any man who is not ruled by law would make the same mistakes as the unrestrained multitude. This can easily be shown, for though there have been many princes, there have been few who were wise and good. I am speaking of rulers who were able to break the bonds that could have controlled their actions. These do not include those kings who arose in Egypt in remote antiquity when that country was governed by laws, nor do they include those who arose in Sparta, nor those of present-day France, for that kingdom is controlled by laws more fully than any other present kingdom of which we have information. Such kings as come to hold power under a constitution are not to be counted among those whose individual nature we have to consider in order to discover whether it is like that of the multitude. Otherwise we should have to compare kings regulated by law with a multitude similarly regulated, and we would find the same virtues in both. We would also find the multitude, as in the case of the Roman people, neither haughtily dominant nor humbly submissive; for as long as the Roman republic remained uncorrupted, the people did not serve humbly or dominate arrogantly. On the contrary, they kept their places honorably with their own laws and their own officials. And when it was necessary to rise up against some powerful individual, they did so, as in the case of Manlius, of the Decemvirs,[3] and of others who sought to oppress them. And when it was necessary to obey a dictator or the consuls for public good, they did so. And if they mourned the dead Manlius Capitolinus, there is no cause for surprise, since it was his virtues they mourned; and these were such that the memory of them aroused compassion in everyone and they would have been capable of producing the same effect in a prince, since all writers agree that virtue is praised and admired even in one's enemies. But even if all their mourning had been enough to return Manlius from the dead, the Roman people would have passed the same judgment upon him, again taking him from prison and again sentencing him to death. Nonetheless, there have been princes reputed wise who put people to death and then mourned their loss bitterly, as Alexander the Great mourned Clitus and other friends, and as Herod mourned Mariamne.[4] Yet what our historian says about the nature of multitudes he does not apply to those that were regulated by law, as the Roman people were, but to unrestrained multitudes like those of Syracuse who committed the same mistakes that enraged men commit, mistakes like those of Alexander and Herod which have already been referred to. Therefore, the nature of multitudes is no more to be blamed than the nature of princes, for all err equally when all can err without distinction. As evidence of this, besides the examples already cited, there are many to be found among the Roman emperors and among other tyrants and rulers who displayed as much inconstancy and fickleness as was ever seen in any multitude.

My conclusion, then, is contrary to the common opinion, which claims that the people, when in power, are variable, unstable, and ungrateful; and I affirm that these faults are no more common to them than to individual princes. Now, if someone were to accuse people and princes together, he could be right; but if he were to exclude princes, he would deceive himself; for a populace that has power and is well regulated by laws will be as stable, as prudent, and as grateful as a prince or, indeed, more so than a reputedly wise prince. On the other hand, a prince who is not restrained by laws will show more ingratitude and be more fickle and imprudent than the people. Differences between the conduct of the multitude and the conduct of princes do not derive from differences in their nature, that being the same in both (though if there be some superiority either way, it will be found on the side of the people); rather, they derive from differences in their respect for the laws under which they live.

Those who study the Roman people will note that for four hundred years they hated the name of king and loved the glory and common welfare of their country, and they will note a host of examples testifying to both of these attitudes. Now, if someone were to cite their ingratitude toward Scipio,[5] I would call attention to what I have already said at length about this matter, where I demonstrate that the people show less ingratitude than princes. As to prudence and stability, I say that the people are more prudent, more stable, and more judicious than princes. And it is not without reason that the voice of the people has been likened to the voice of God,[6] for popular opinion is amazingly reliable in its prognostications, so much so that the people would seem to have hidden powers by which to foresee their future ills and triumphs. As to judging things, if they hear two equally skillful public speakers present opposing views, rarely will they fail to choose the better argument or show an incapacity to fathom the truth of what they hear. And if they err in matters involving courage or advantage, as I said before,[7] so too does a prince often err in matters involving his passions, and these are more intense than those of the people. Again, in the election of public officials we note that they make far better choices than princes do. It is never possible to persuade the people to bestow authority upon a man of disreputable and corrupt habits, while a prince can be so persuaded in a thousand different ways. Moreover, when the people begin to look upon a thing with horror, they will persevere in that attitude for many centuries, but princes will not do so. On these last two points I shall let the Roman people suffice as evidence. Through many centuries and in a host of elections of consuls and Tribunes, they made no more than four choices they had cause to regret; and, as I said, they so much despised the name of king that no debt of obligation to any citizen was enough to save him from merited punishment if he attempted to usurp that name. Then, too, in cities where the people rule, we see extraordinary progress achieved in a scant few years, far greater than any ever achieved under a prince, as witness Rome after the expulsion of her kings, and Athens after her liberation from Pisistratus.[8] This cannot be the result of anything but the fact that popular governments are superior to those of princes. And I will not grant that all of what Livy has to say in the passage referred to or in any other is sufficient to oppose my views, for if we compare all the disorders chargeable to the people with all the disorders chargeable to princes, and all the glorious achievements of the people with all those of princes, we will find that in glory as in goodness the people are far superior. If princes are indeed superior to the people in enacting laws, in organizing civil governments, in setting up new statutes and ordinances, then doubtless the people are so superior in maintaining what has been instituted that they increase the glory of those who instituted them.

In short, to conclude this subject, I say that republics have endured for many years just as princely states have, and both have needed to be regulated by laws. A prince who is free to do as he pleases is unreasonable, and a people that is free to do as it pleases is not wise. If we consider princes restricted by laws and a people bound by laws, we will find greater qualities in the people than in the princes. If we consider them both when unrestrained by laws, we will find the people making fewer and less weighty errors than princes, and possessing weightier remedies for them. A corrupt and disorderly multitude can be spoken to by some worthy person and can easily be brought around to the right way, but a bad prince cannot be spoken to by anyone, and the only remedy for his case is cold steel. From this we may conjecture as to which is susceptible to the graver illness; for if words are enough to cure the people's illness and only steel will cure that of a prince, no one will fail to conclude that a graver cure argues a graver defect. When the people are without restraints, their follies need not be feared, nor need there be so much apprehension about immediate ills as about those that may ensue, for out of such confusion a tyrant may emerge. But in the case of a bad prince the contrary is true, for it is immediate ills that are to be feared, while the future will embody hope, and men will be able to persuade themselves that the prince's bad conduct will clear the way for liberty. Note the difference between these two. It is the same as the difference between what is and what is yet to be. The cruelties of the multitude are directed against those whom they fear will usurp their common welfare; those of a prince are directed against those whom he fears will usurp his own well-being. Opinions in dispraise of the people originate in the fact that everyone can speak ill of them freely and without fear even while they are the rulers. Of princes one can only speak on any occasion with a host of fears and precautions.

Now, since my subject draws me to it, I do not think it would be unsuitable to consider in the next chapter what sort of alliances are the most trustworthy, whether those formed with republics or those made with princes.[9]

BOOK TWO

2. THE PEOPLE THE ROMANS HAD TO FIGHT, AND HOW OBSTINATELY THEY DEFENDED THEIR FREEDOM

T O THE difficulty the Romans encountered in overcoming neighboring peoples and some far-off provinces, nothing contributed so much as the love of liberty which the people of those times had. So obstinately did they defend it that they could never have been subjugated except by unusual prowess, for by many examples we know the dangers they faced to preserve it or regain it. From the reading of history we also learn how harmful servitude was to peoples and cities. And though in our own day there is only one country that can be said to have free cities,[1] in ancient times there were many people enjoying abundant freedom in all countries. In Italy at the time of which we are now speaking, we note that, beginning at the Alps which separate Tuscany from Lombardy and going southward to the toe, all the people were free. These included the Tuscans,[2] the Romans, the Samnites, and many others who occupied the region. Nor do we ever encounter any mention of kings except for those who reigned in Rome and except for the Tuscan Porsenna about whom history is silent regarding the extinction of his line. But it is clear that when the Romans began their siege of Veii the Tuscans were free. And so much did they enjoy their liberty, and in fact hate the name of prince, that when the Veienti chose a king as their defender against the Romans and sent to the Tuscans for aid, the latter, after much deliberation, refused to send it for as long as the Veienti had a king, because they judged it unwise to defend a nation that had already submitted to someone.

It is easy to understand whence this love of liberty derives among people, for experience shows that no city ever grew in dominion or wealth except when it was free. And it is indeed a wonder to realize how great Athens became within a century after it had thrown off the tyranny established by Pisistratus.[3] But it is even more extraordinary to note the greatness which Rome attained after she was free of her kings. The reason is easy to understand, for it is not the welfare of individuals but the common welfare that makes cities great. And doubtless this common welfare cannot be pursued except in republics because they undertake whatever action may be needed to promote it. However harmful its pursuit may be to this or that individual, those who stand to gain are so numerous that they can pursue it in spite of the few who may be harmed.

The contrary is true where there is a prince. In such a case the things which are of advantage to him more often than not are harmful to the city, and the things which are of advantage to the city are harmful to him. Thus, wherever tyranny replaces freedom, the least that can happen is that the city will no longer increase in either power or wealth. Most often, indeed always, it will decline. And if by chance a very capable tyrant appears by whose courage and military skill the city's territories are increased, it will not be a gain for the republic, but only for him, because he cannot advance any of those good and valiant citizens over whom he tyrannizes, for they will then become dangerous. Moreover, as to any lands he may conquer, he cannot make them subject or tributary to the city of which he is lord, for he gains no advantage by making it stronger. His advantage lies in keeping the state disunited, each part of it directly subject to him. Thus he, and not his city, profits from his conquests. Anyone who wishes to confirm this view with a host of additional arguments may read Xenophon's treatise entitled *On Tyranny*.[4]

It is no wonder then that the people of antiquity despised tyrants, loved living in freedom, and exalted the name of liberty as they did when Hieronymus, the grandson of Hiero of Syracuse, was slain in that city.[5] When the news reached the army, which was stationed not far from Syracuse, the soldiers became enraged and began to take up arms against the slayers; but when they heard that the people were shouting liberty in

Syracuse, beguiled by that word, they became calm. It is also
no wonder that the people take extraordinary vengeance upon
those who deprive them of their freedom. Of this there have
been many instances, of which I would like to mention only
one. It took place in the Greek city of Corcyra during the
Peloponnesian War.[6] Greece was then divided into two parties,
one headed by the Athenians, the other by the Spartans, with
the result that many cities were internally divided, one faction
favoring Sparta, the other Athens. At that time the nobles of
Corcyra rose up and deprived the people of their liberty. Aided
by the Athenians however, the people soon regained the upper
hand and, having seized all the nobles of the city, they locked
them up in a prison large enough to hold them all. From there,
under pretense of sending them off to various places of exile,
they led them out eight or ten at a time and, using many cruel
torments, slew them. When those who were still left in the
prison became aware of this, they decided to use every possible means to escape such an ignominious death and, having
armed themselves as best they could, they defended the prison
entrance against those who sought to enter. At this, the people,
drawn to the scene by the noise of fighting, tore down the upper sections of the building and smothered the nobles beneath
the ruins. Many other similarly amazing and horrible events
occurred in that land. So we see that a freedom that has been
lost is avenged with far more fury than one that has only been
threatened.

Having wondered why people in those ancient times were
fonder of liberty than they are today, I have concluded that it is
the same reason that explains why men are now less coura-
geous than they were then. I believe it is to be explained by the
difference between our education and theirs and by the difference of religion upon which it is based. Our religion, having
shown us the truth and the true way, has caused us to have less
esteem for worldly honor, whereas the pagans, because they
believed worldly honor to be the highest good, showed greater
fierceness in their actions. This is demonstrated in many of
their customs as compared to ours, beginning with the splendor
of their sacrifices and the humbleness of ours. There is more

gentleness than magnificence in some of ours, and nothing that is fierce or vigorous. Their ceremonies lacked neither pomp nor magnificence, but they added the extremely bloody and fierce act of sacrifice in which hordes of animals were killed. This savage aspect of them tended to make the participants savage too. Moreover, ancient religion exalted none but such men as had attained great worldly glory, like commanders of armies and rulers of republics.

Our religion has tended to glorify humble and contemplative men rather than men of action. Moreover, it has claimed that the highest good lies in humility, humbleness, and contempt of human things. Their religion claimed that it lay in greatness of spirit, physical strength, and in all those things tending to make men brave. If our religion demands courage of a man, it demands it so that he may be able to suffer rather than do anything bold. This way of life, then, seems to have made the world soft and given it as prey to the wicked who can assuredly manage it, since the generality of men, questing after paradise, thinks more of putting up with blows than of avenging them. And though the world seems to have become effeminate and heaven to have become disarmed, doubtless this is primarily due to the baseness of men who have interpreted our religion according to the promptings of indolence rather than the promptings of vigor. For if we considered how it permits us to exalt and defend our country, we would realize that it desires us to love it and honor it as well, and bids us prepare ourselves to be such as can defend it.

This kind of education and these false interpretations explain why we no longer see as many republics in the world as there were in ancient times, and why people consequently do not have such love of liberty as they had then, though I rather believe a greater cause to be that the Roman Empire destroyed all the republics and free forms of civic life. Even though the Empire later disintegrated, the cities were unable to reform and reorganize their civic life except in a very few cases. But whatever the cause, in every part of the world, whatever its size, the Romans found leagues of republics fully armed and very determined in the defense of their freedom. This shows that without rare and extreme valor the Roman people would have been unable to overcome them.

As to particular instances that bear this out, I shall cite but one, that of the Samnites, who, marvelous to relate,—and Titus Livy admits it—proved themselves so powerful, so valiant in arms, that they were able to oppose the Romans for a span of forty-six years, down to the time of the Consul Papirius Cursor (son of the first Papirius) despite the routs, the destruction of cities, and the massacres their land suffered.[7] This is all the more impressive when we see how that land which had held so many people and cities is now almost uninhabited. At that time it was so well ordered, so strong, that it would have proved unconquerable to all but Roman might and valor.

It is easy to account for the prosperous civic life of that time and for the lack of it now, for it all comes from the fact that they lived in freedom and we live in servitude. As I said before, cities and states that enjoy full freedom prosper greatly. They have larger populations because marriage is easier there and more desirable; for men will willingly have children when they believe they can provide for them, when they do not fear they will be deprived of their patrimony, and when they recognize that their young will not only grow up free men instead of slaves, but that, with ability, they may also become leaders. In such states riches multiply abundantly, both those produced by agriculture and those produced by industry, for everyone willingly increases his property and goods if he believes that he will be allowed to enjoy them. In such circumstances men compete with each other in providing both private and public benefits, with the result that both increase remarkably.

The contrary of all this is true for states that live in servitude, and the harsher their servitude the more reduced is their prosperity. And of harsh servitudes the harshest is to be in subjection to a republic. The first reason for this is that it is the most enduring kind and offers no hope of release. The second is that the aim of a republic is to enervate and weaken its subject lands in order to increase its own prosperity. Such is not the aim of a conquering prince unless he is a barbarian who destroys countries and lays waste all the works of civilized man, as oriental princes do. But if he has common human principles, he will most often have equal regard for all his subject cities and will let them keep their industries and nearly all their institutions. Thus, though they may not advance as free cities do, they will not decline as enslaved ones do. I speak of those in subjection to a foreigner, for I spoke earlier of those in subjection to a citizen.

Anyone considering all that has been said, then, will not be surprised at the power of the Samnites when they were free and at their weakness after they were subjugated. Titus Livy assures us of this in many places, especially where he recounts the war with Hannibal. Here he tells us that when the Samnites were being oppressed by a Roman legion stationed in Nola, they sent emissaries to ask Hannibal for assistance. In their address they explained that they had fought the Romans for a hundred years with their own troops and their own commanders, that they had many times resisted two consular armies and two consuls at the same time, and that now they were reduced to such conditions that they could scarcely defend themselves from a little Roman legion stationed in Nola.

BOOK THREE

21. How It Happened That Hannibal Gained the Same Results in Italy As Scipio Did in Spain by Contrary Means

I THINK that some people may be surprised when they see a certain general, despite a contrary line of conduct, achieving the same results as those who acted as I have just described.[1] It may seem that victories do not depend upon the methods that have been mentioned. Indeed, it may seem that such methods bring neither more power nor better fortune, since fame and glory may be attained by the very opposite methods. Now, so as not to depart from the men I have been speaking of and so as to clarify the point I wish to make, I say that Scipio, as we know, entered Spain and gained the friendship of that province, the love and admiration of its people, by using mercy and kindness. In contrast we saw Hannibal attain the same results in Italy as Scipio did in Spain by using entirely opposite methods—that is, cruelty, violence, rapine, and every sort of faithlessness, for all the cities of Italy bolted to him and all the people obeyed him.

If we try to discover how this came about, we will find several reasons. The first is that men—those who are well off as much as those who are not—desire novelty. For, as was said before—and it is true—men grow weary of good conditions and become dejected with bad ones. This desire, then, opens the doors of a province to anyone introducing change. If he is a foreigner, people will flock to him; if he is a native, they will surround him and lend him support and favor so that, whatever his line of conduct, he will have great success in such a place. Besides, men are moved by two principal things—by love and by fear. Consequently, they are commanded as well by someone who wins their affection as by someone who arouses their fear. Indeed, in most instances the one who arouses their fear gains more of a following and is more readily obeyed than the one who wins their affection.

But so long as he has ability and so long as his ability is respected, it matters little to a general whether he pursues one of these policies or the other. For when the ability is great, as it was in the case of Hannibal and Scipio, it cancels out all those errors which come about through winning too much affection or arousing too much fear. But both of these methods can produce difficulties capable of ruining a leader. For the person who desires too much to be loved, any slight departure from the right course will bring contempt, while for the person who desires too much to be feared, any slight exceeding of due measure will bring hatred. Yet to hold a middle course is impossible because our nature does not allow it. Therefore it is necessary to compensate for excesses by exercising unusual ability, as Hannibal and Scipio did. Nevertheless, we may note that both were harmed by their conduct, yet both were successful.

Their success has already been dealt with. As to the harm in the case of Scipio, it was that his soldiers, together with some of his allies, rebelled against him. This could have had no other cause but his failure to arouse fear, for men are so restless that, once a little door is provided for their ambition, they quickly forget all the affection they had bestowed on their leader because of his kindness, just as these soldiers and allies did. Thus, in order to remedy the difficulty, Scipio was compelled to use some of the cruelty he had shunned. As to Hannibal, there is no specific instance in which his cruelty and faithlessness did him harm. But it may be supposed that Naples and many other cities that remained loyal to the Romans did so because of their fear of him. At any rate, it is certain that his impious conduct made him more hateful to the Romans than any enemy their republic had ever had before. Thus, though they had been willing to warn Pyrrhus about the man who proposed to poison him even while he was with his army in Italy, they never forgave Hannibal even after he was disarmed and his troops were scattered, and they brought about his death.[2] These disadvantages accrued to Hannibal, then, because he was impious, faithless, and cruel, but on the other hand they gave him a very great advantage which all the writers have admired. It is that though his army was composed of different races, no dissension ever arose to set them against each other or against him. This could only have derived from the terror his person aroused, which was so great that, combined with his renowned ability, it sufficed to keep his soldiers quiet and united.

I conclude, therefore, that it does not much matter which method a general adopts so long as he possesses great ability to go along with either the one or the other; for, as I said before, both methods are defective and dangerous unless corrected by exceptional skill. Now if Hannibal and Scipio achieved the same results by opposite means—the one detestable, the other praiseworthy, I do not think it amiss to speak of two Roman citizens who attained equal glory by opposite but equally praiseworthy means.[3]

41. THAT ONE'S COUNTRY OUGHT TO BE DEFENDED, WHETHER WITH SHAME OR GLORY, BY WHATEVER MEANS POSSIBLE

AS I said above,[1] the Consul and the Roman army were being besieged by the Samnites, who had imposed very shameful conditions upon their surrender (this involved passing under the yoke and returning disarmed to Rome). The Consul was astonished at this and the army was in despair, but Lucius Lentulus, the Roman legate, expressed it as his opinion that no proposal by which their country could be saved should be rejected. Since the survival of Rome depended upon the survival of that particular army, he felt that it should be saved by whatever means possible, whether shameful or glorious; for if the army were saved there would be time to erase the shame, but if it were not saved, even if it perished gloriously, Rome and her liberty would be lost. Consequently, his counsel was accepted.

This decision deserves to be noted and adopted by every citizen who may be called upon to advise his country; for where the well-being of one's country is at all in question, no consideration of justice or injustice, of mercy or cruelty, of honor or shame must be allowed to enter in at all. Indeed, every other consideration having been put aside, that course of action alone which will save the life and liberty of the country ought to be wholeheartedly pursued. The French have adopted this policy in both word and deed to protect the majesty of their king and the might of their kingdom, for they will hear no opinion with so much impatience as that which describes a certain course of action as being disgraceful to the king. They assert that their king is immune to shame in any action he undertakes, whether successful or not; for, win or lose, they say, it is always a kingly action.

CHRONOLOGY

<table>
<tr><td>1469</td><td>May 3. Machiavelli born in Florence.</td></tr>
<tr><td>1492</td><td>Lorenzo de' Medici (The Magnificent) dies.</td></tr>
</table>

1469   May 3. Machiavelli born in Florence.

1492   Lorenzo de' Medici (The Magnificent) dies.

      Alexander VI (Rodrigo Borgia) becomes Pope.

1494   Charles VIII of France invades Italy. Piero de' Medici is driven out of Florence.

      Pisa becomes independent after nearly a century of subjection to Florence.

      A new Florentine constitution is adopted, largely the work of Savonarola.

      Battle of Fornovo (Il Taro); the French drive through an Italian army and make good their escape from Italy.

1495   Florence begins efforts to regain Pisa.

1498   Savonarola is put to death by hanging, and his body is burned.

      Louis XII becomes King of France.

      Machiavelli is appointed Secretary to the Signoria.

1499   Louis XII invades Italy.

      Cesare Borgia begins the conquest of Romagna.

1500   Machiavelli's first mission to France.

1501   Cesare Borgia is named Duke of Romagna.

1502   Pier Soderini becomes Gonfalonier of Florence for life.

1503   Pope Alexander VI dies; Pius III succeeds him, then dies less than a month later.

      Julius II (Giuliano della Rovere) becomes Pope.

1504   Machiavelli's second mission to France.

      Cesare Borgia surrenders Romagna to Julius II and is then sent to Spain as a prisoner.

1506   Machiavelli begins work on establishing a citizen militia.

1507   Machiavelli is sent on a mission to Emperor Maximilian.

1508   Machiavelli is put in charge of operations against Pisa.

The League of Cambray (Louis XII, Ferdinand of Aragon, Julius II, Emperor Maximilian) is formed to attack Venice.

1509   Pisa surrenders to the Florentines.

Battle of Vailà (Agnadello) results in defeat of Venice by the League of Cambray.

1510   Machiavelli's third mission to France; returns and resumes work on the militia.

1511   Machiavelli's fourth mission to France.

The Holy League (Julius II, Venice, Ferdinand of Spain) is formed to expel the French from Italy.

1512   Battle of Ravenna. The French are triumphant over the Holy League, but are forced to withdraw from Italy at the approach of a Swiss army in the pay of Pope Julius II. Spanish troops accompanied by the de' Medici enter Florentine territory, demand the deposition of Soderini. When the request is refused, they attack Prato, enter the city, and sack it. Two days later Soderini resigns. Six weeks later Machiavelli is discharged from office.

1513   Leo X (Giovanni de' Medici) becomes Pope.

Machiavelli retires to his farm near San Casciano, works on *The Discourses* and completes *The Prince*.

1515   Francis I becomes King of France.

1519   Leo X applies to Machiavelli for political advice.

1520   Machiavelli writes *The Art of War* and *The Life of Castruccio*.

Begins his *History of Florence* under a commission from the officers of the *Studio pubblico*.

1524   Machiavelli's play *Mandragola* is printed.

1526   Machiavelli employed by Clement VII to inspect the fortifications of Florence.

1527   June 20. Machiavelli dies.

NOTES TO *THE PRINCE*

DEDICATION

1. Duke of Urbino and grandson of Lorenzo the Magnificent (1449–1492). Originally, *The Prince* had been dedicated to Giuliano de' Medici (Duke of Nemours and son of Lorenzo the Magnificent) who died in 1516.

2. An allusion to his unhappiness at being excluded from political office and tacitly expressing the hope of being employed by the Medici party, perhaps Machiavelli's chief motive in writing the present work.

CHAPTER 1

1. Francesco Sforza (1401–1466), a soldier by profession, succeeded in becoming Duke of Milan in 1450 through the aid of the Venetians.

2. Ferdinand II (1452–1516), called the Catholic, added the Kingdom of Naples to his possessions in 1501 and Sicily in 1504.

3. Fortune is generally used by Machiavelli to mean the nature of circumstances which, if favorable, are to be exploited for one's own ends and, if unfavorable, are to be overcome or minimized by appropriate action. It is not intended merely to imply luck and, whether favorable or unfavorable, it is never an excuse for inaction.

    "Ability" is generally used to translate Machiavelli's *virtù*. A key word in *The Prince* and *The Discourses*, it implies physical and mental capacity—intelligence, skill, courage, vigor—in short, all those personal qualities that are needed for the attainment of one's own ends. The term almost invariably carries no implication of virtue in the moral sense.

CHAPTER 2

1. Almost certainly a reference to *The Discourses*, which were put aside in 1513 to make way for the present work and were later resumed.

2. Ercole d'Este I was defeated by the Venetians in 1482, but nearly all his territories were restored to him in 1484. Pope Julius II (d. 1513) made numerous attempts—all unsuccessful—to deprive Alfonso d'Este I of Ferrara.

3. Dentations: stones projecting from the surface of a wall for the support of subsequent abutting structures.

CHAPTER 3

1. Duke Ludovico il Moro was driven from Milan by the troops of Louis XII in 1499. However, thanks to uprisings against the French within the city and the aid of Swiss mercenaries, he was able to regain it early in the following year. But he held it for barely a month when he was again driven out by the French.

2. Louis retained possession of Milan until 1512. In that year the operations of the Holy League (Pope Julius II, Ferdinand the Catholic, and the Venetians) forced him to withdraw his troops from the peninsula.

3. Mohamet II conquered Constantinople in 1453 and made it his capital.

4. The Etolian League joined the Romans in opposing Philip V of Macedon and the Achaean League in the First Macedonian War (215–205 B.C.).

5. The events somewhat loosely referred to here are as follows: in 197 B.C., the Romans defeated Philip V of Macedon at Cynocephalae and forced him to surrender the Greek cities he had acquired after the First Macedonian War. In 191, Antiochus III of Syria invaded Greece at the invitation of the Etolians but was driven back into Asia Minor by the Romans, who this time were supported by Philip V and the Achaean League. In concluding peace, the

Romans did not increase the power of their recent allies; instead, they preferred to enlarge the Kingdom of Pergamum as a counterweight to their future ambitions.

6. Probably a reference to the policy of Pier Soderini, the leader of the Florentine government during most of Machiavelli's political career.

7. I.e., not of Charles VIII (who invaded Italy in 1494) but of Louis XII (whose first expedition came five years later).

8. Louis had hereditary claims on both the Duchy of Milan and the Kingdom of Naples. For supporting him, the Venetians had been promised Cremona and Ghiaradadda.

9. His brief appearance in Italy had entirely disrupted the political balance of the peninsula without bringing him any gains.

10. Though Romagna had long been divided into a number of independent and semi-independent states, Pope Alexander VI claimed it as a dominion of the Church and wished to establish his authority—or that of his son Cesare Borgia— over it. To this end he entered into a secret agreement with Louis in 1498, the chief terms of which were: (1) that Cesare Borgia was to be made Duke of Valentinois; (2) that he was to be provided with troops for the occupation of Romagna; (3) that Louis was to be granted a divorce (from Jeanne of France, daughter of Louis XI) so as to be free to marry Anne (widow of Charles VIII) and acquire Brittany as her dowry; (4) that Louis's chief adviser, George d'Amboise, was to become Cardinal of Rouen.

11. After the conquest of Milan in 1499, Louis withdrew from Italy, leaving his viceroy in charge. He returned in 1502 to prepare for the conquest of Naples (*see* Note 8 above). By that date Cesare Borgia had become master of most of Romagna and was threatening intervention in Tuscany, an action which Louis opposed, since the Florentines were his allies.

12. By the terms of the Treaty of Granada (November, 1500), Louis had agreed to partition the Kingdom of Naples with Ferdinand of Spain.

13. In fact, the joint French and Spanish venture into Naples did result in conflict between them, and after the Battle of the Garigliano (December, 1503), the Spanish became sole masters of Naples.

14. That is, he helped Cesare Borgia to extinguish the smaller powers of Romagna; he thereby increased the power of the Church, which was already strong; he allowed Ferdinand of Spain to become involved in the affairs of Italy.

15. In joining the League of Cambray (1508), Louis allied himself with the Pope (now Julius II), Ferdinand, the Emperor Maximilian, and others in bringing about the defeat of Venice at the Battle of Vailà (May, 1509), by which Venice lost most of her mainland possessions.

CHAPTER 4

1. Alexander invaded Asia Minor in 334 B.C., defeated Darius at Gaugamela in 331, and reached India in 327. He died in 323, scarcely eleven years after starting off on his expedition.

2. Alexander's successors—his generals—began to fight over the spoils of his empire soon after his death, and ultimately partitioned it among themselves.

3. Sanjaks: territories or provinces ruled by a governor appointed by the sultan.

4. Apparently Machiavelli is implying that the pre-Roman tribal chieftains of Spain and Gaul (and later ones like Vercingetorix, who rebelled against Caesar), as well as the hereditary rulers of some of the Greek confederate states, had a political status similar to that of the feudal French barons.

5. Pyrrhus, King of Epirus, brought an army into Sicily in 278 B.C., but met with little real success. Machiavelli attributes his failure to the fact that the Greek city states of Sicily, unlike the Persian and Ottoman empires, were not under direct absolute rule.

CHAPTER 5

1. That is, to destroy its political and civil structure.

2. At the end of the Peloponnesian War, Sparta required Athens to accept an oligarchy composed of thirty pro-Spartan Athenians (the so-called thirty tyrants). Democracy was restored, however, in the following year. Sparta imposed a similar oligarchy upon Thebes in 382 B.C. This was driven out three years later.

3. The Romans destroyed Capua in 211 B.C., Carthage in 146, Numantia in 133. Thereafter they remained in Roman hands.

4. Roman intervention in Greek affairs began during the Second Punic War, in which Philip V of Macedon sided with Hannibal. It continued sporadically through the four so-called Macedonian Wars (215–146 B.C.). The Romans frequently tried to establish aristocratic or oligarchic governments in the Greek states, but with little lasting success. Corinth was destroyed in 146 B.C. and her inhabitants were sold into slavery. Thereafter Greece was a Roman province. *See also* Chapter 3, Notes 4 and 5.

5. Pisa became a Florentine possession in 1405 and remained so until 1494 (when Charles VIII of France invaded Italy). It was not reduced to submission again until 1509. Machiavelli himself played an important part in bringing this about.

CHAPTER 6

1. *See* Chapter 1, Note 3 and Chapter 25.

2. Cyrus: founder of the Persian Empire (558–529 B.C.); Romulus: legendary founder of Rome; Theseus: legendary hero of Athens. This intermingling of Biblical, legendary, and historical figures (all accepted as genuinely historical by the author) does not in any way weaken Machiavelli's point here if, as some commentators have done, they are all taken to represent symbolic political types.

3. Fra' (Friar) Girolamo Savonarola: a Dominican born in Ferrara, he was sent to preach in Florence in 1492. His sermons, fiery and persuasive, soon gained him a large following throughout the city. The descent of Charles VIII into Italy (which it was believed he had prophesied) and the establishment of the republican government after the expulsion of Piero de' Medici (1494) brought him into political prominence. The constitution then adopted was substantially his own work, and for a few years thereafter little was done in the city without his consent. His strenuous efforts to reform the city's morals aroused both enthusiasm and animosity. But it was largely because of his outspoken criticism of Pope Alexander VI that he was excommunicated and later imprisoned and tortured. In 1498, after a trial for heresy conducted by two Apostolic Commissioners sent from Rome, he was hanged and burned in the Piazza della Signoria.

4. Hiero II of Syracuse, publicly elected king after he had defeated the Mamertines. Initially allied with Carthage in the First Punic War (264–241 B.C.), he later became a staunch and faithful ally of the Romans. *See* Chapter 13.

5. Justin, *Historiarum Philippicarum libri* XLIV, XXIII, 4.

CHAPTER 7

1. Darius I, King of Persia (521–485 B.C.), divided his kingdom into twenty or more satrapies.

2. The reference is to the Roman emperors (discussed at length in Chapter 19) who gained the purple by bribery or by outright purchase from the Praetorian commanders.

3. For Francesco Sforza, *see* Chapter 1, Note 1. For Cesare Borgia, *see* Chapter 3, Notes 10 and 11. As will be seen from what follows, Cesare Borgia was the very type of the new prince whom Machiavelli had in mind. The events described—some of which the author himself witnessed—cover a span of less than five years, 1498–1503.

4. I.e., the simultaneous illness of his father and himself. *See* Note 16 below.

5. In Romagna the two small states of Forlì and Pesaro were under the protection of Ludovico il Moro (son of Francesco Sforza), while Faenza and Rimini were under the protection of Venice.

6. The very numerous Orsini and Colonna families had been prominent in Roman affairs for centuries. Usually the leaders of rival factions, in possession of extensive land holdings and numerous fortresses in and around Rome, they constituted an almost perpetual threat to papal authority and were therefore the Pope's traditional enemies. Like many other Italian barons or princelings of the time, they were often captains of mercenary armies.

7. *See* Chapter 3, Notes 8 and 10. Louis's marriage to Anne of Brittany also gave him title to the Duchy of Milan.

8. Borgia was created Duke of Romagna in 1501.

9. Paolo Orsini was reluctant to support the attack on Bologna for fear that Borgia's power, if sufficient, would ultimately be the undoing of the captains he was now dependent upon.

10. Louis sent troops to the defense of Florence.

11. In October, 1502, Borgia's hired captains met at La Magione and formed a conspiracy to frustrate his further ambitions. They agreed to keep possession of territories they had conquered in his name, to encourage rebellion in other Borgia territories, to form an army for their common defense, and to seek allies. The revolt of Urbino and the disorders of Romagna were the immediate result. Borgia countered by obtaining more French troops, and this forced the conspirators to make peace overtures. The conditions Borgia offered were deceptively generous. The conspirators agreed to restore all lost territories and to continue in his service.

12. In December, 1502, Borgia suddenly dismissed his French troops.

13. Believing that they had become entirely reconciled with Borgia, the former conspirators proceeded to fulfill their

agreement and then joined him in Senigallia. There Borgia had them seized. Two of the captains (Vitellozzo Vitelli and Oliverotto da Fermo) were strangled immediately. Two others (the Duke of Gravina and Paolo Orsini) met the same fate a few weeks later.

14. *See* Note 10 above.

15. *See* Chapter 3, Notes 12 and 13. The French had recently suffered serious reverses and were facing defeat. Alexander and his son were therefore planning to abandon them and join the Spaniards.

16. On August 5, 1503, following a dinner at the residence of a cardinal, the Pope and his son became seriously ill. Less than two weeks later the Pope was dead, and Cesare did not recover until September. Meanwhile the College of Cardinals was meeting in conclave to elect a new pope, a French army was advancing south to the relief of Gaeta, and the Spanish forces to the south were assembling to meet it.

17. Survivors and relatives of the conspirators of La Magione. *See* Note 11 above.

18. Pius III succeeded Alexander VI but survived only a month, and was in turn succeeded (November 1, 1503) by Giuliano della Rovere, who took the name Julius II.

19. Some of the motives these men had for opposing Cesare Borgia may be deduced from the following facts: Giuliano della Rovere had been one of Alexander's chief rivals for the tiara in 1492. Later Cesare had expelled his brother from the lordship of Senigallia. Raffaello Riario was related to both Giuliano della Rovere and Caterina Sforza of Forlì, whom Cesare had also deposed. Ascanio Sforza was the brother of Ludovico il Moro, who had been driven from Milan by Cesare's ally, Louis XII. For Giovanni Colonna, *see* Note 6 above.

CHAPTER 8

1. In Chapter 6 Machiavelli deals with examples of men who became rulers by means of their ability; in Chapter 7 he deals with those who became rulers by means of the fortunes of others. Here and in Chapter 9, he deals with the two remaining methods of becoming a ruler, which are briefly defined in this paragraph.

2. Agathocles was King of Syracuse from 317 to 289 B.C. For a time he ruled nearly all of Sicily.

3. *See* Chapter 7, Notes 11 and 13.

CHAPTER 9

1. Or more precisely, monarchy, democracy, or anarchy. *See The Discourses* One, II.

2. Nabis was tyrant of Sparta between 207 and 192 B.C. He proposed a redistribution of land in order to gain popular favor.

3. The Gracchi, Tiberius and Caius, Tribunes of the people in 133 and 123 B.C., respectively, introduced agrarian reforms in the interests of the lower classes and fell victims to the wrath of the Senate.

   Giorgio Scali, one of the leaders of the Plebeian party, lost the favor of the people through his insolence, and was beheaded in 1382, after attempting to rescue a friend from prison by force.

CHAPTER 10

1. Treated in Chapter 6, developed further in Chapters 12 and 13.

2. Most of the cities and states of Germany were nominally under the authority of the Holy Roman Emperor (Maximilian, 1493–1519). But in Machiavelli's day—and even long before—the emperor's power was insufficient to make good his lawful claims.

CHAPTER 11

1. The French monarch referred to is Louis XII, who was forced to withdraw from Italy in 1512 after the Battle of Ravenna as a consequence of the actions of the Holy League led by Pope Julius II (1503–1513). The reference to the Venetians relates to events that had occurred earlier—the successful operations of the League of Cambray by which Julius had managed to use the French to subdue the Venetians in 1509. *See* Chapter 3, Notes 2 and 15.

2. That is, before 1494.

3. Venice sought to add Ferrara to its dominions in 1482. After some initial successes, it was forced to disgorge its gains when a league (chiefly Florence, Naples, Milan) was organized to oppose its expansion.

4. *See* Chapter 7, Note 6.

5. Pope Sixtus IV (1471–1484), uncle of Pope Julius II, had been very vigorous in promoting the temporal interests of the Church and of his family.

6. For the French invasion of 1499 and the exploits of Duke Valentino (Cesare Borgia), *see* Chapter 7 and notes.

7. That is, chiefly by the sale of ecclesiastical offices.

8. The major aims of Pope Julius II were: the territorial aggrandizement of the Church (hence the conquest of Bologna in 1506 and the defeat of the Venetians in 1509), and the expulsion of the French from Italian soil (hence the formation of the Holy League referred to in Note 1 above).

9. Pope Leo X (1513–1521), uncle of Lorenzo de' Medici, to whom *The Prince* was dedicated. These lines were written shortly after the Pope's election.

CHAPTER 12

1. The same judgment is expressed in *The Discourses* One, IV.

2. Auxiliaries: troops borrowed from an ally.

3. When Charles VIII met only the scantiest resistance in 1494, Pope Alexander VI was led to say that the French had come with chalk in their hands to mark their lodgings.

4. The remark was attributed to Savonarola. *See* Chapter 6, Note 3.

5. At the end of the First Punic War (241 B.C.), the Carthaginian troops just returned from Sicily mutinied for their pay and were joined by some of the oppressed African subjects. They were not finally put down until 237, after an enormous struggle.

6. Actually Epaminondas died in 362 B.C. Philip did not become King of Macedonia until 359, and did not occupy Thebes until 338.

7. Filippo Visconti (1412–1447): Francesco Sforza's father-in-law (*see* Chapter 1, Note 1). The Battle of Caravaggio took place in 1448.

8. Muzio Attendolo Sforza, Francesco's father, deserted Giovanna in 1426 and took service with Louis III of Anjou, her rival for the throne of Naples.

9. Giovanni Aucut, or Sir John Hawkwood, an Englishman, captain of the White Company hired by Pisa in 1363 and by Florence in 1375. He remained in the service of Florence until his death in 1394.

10. Followers of Braccio da Montone (d. 1434), a condottiere, or captain of a mercenary army, like the others named here. He occupied Rome in 1417 and was driven out by Muzio Attendolo Sforza.

11. Paolo Vitelli (brother of Vitellozzo Vitelli; *see* Chapter 7, Note 13), was hired by Florence in 1498 in her struggle to regain possession of Pisa. Suspected of treason, he was executed the following year.

12. Venetian efforts to expand on the Italian mainland began in 1339 with the occupation of Treviso.

13. Francesco Bussone, Count of Carmagnuola, another condottiere. Initially successful in his operations against Milan, his inaction in the campaign of 1432 aroused the

suspicions of the Venetians, and he was executed soon after.

14. At the Battle of Vailà (or Agnadello) in 1509, part of the Venetian forces were commanded by Niccolò Orsini, Count of Pitigliano. *See* Chapter 3, Note 15.

15. The facts alluded to here refer chiefly to the period between the death of the Emperor Frederick II (1250) and the second invasion of the Emperor Charles IV (1368). During this period the leading factions of the numerous Italian city states were partisans in the dominant conflict of the era—the conflict between pope and emperor for temporal supremacy. The Guelf faction was usually on the side of the pope, while the Ghibelline faction was usually on the side of the emperor. In most instances the republics (or communes) were Guelf. But long after the conflict between pope and emperor had actually ended, Guelfs and Ghibellines continued to play a part in Italian politics.

16. Alberigo da Conio (d. 1409), founder of the Company of St. George, a mercenary army.

17. That is, Charles VIII, Louis XII, Ferdinand the Catholic, and the Swiss mercenary armies frequently engaged in Italian campaigns.

CHAPTER 13

1. The reference is to the formation of the Holy League in 1511. *See* Chapter 3, Note 2.

2. Immediately following the rout of the Holy League at Ravenna in 1512, twenty thousand Swiss troops, hired by the Pope, entered Italy and drove the victors back into France.

3. The troops, largely Gascons and Swiss hired by Louis XII, mutinied shortly after beginning the assault on Pisa.

4. Emperor John Cantacuzene summoned the Turks in 1353 to help in his dynastic struggles with the Paleologi. When the struggle ended two years later, the Turks stayed on.

5. Already discussed in Chapter 7.

6. *See* Chapter 6, Note 4.

7. I Sam. 17:39.

8. Charles VII (1422–1461) organized the Franc Archers (i.e., infantry) in 1448, successfully ended the Hundred Years' War in 1453, leaving only Calais in English hands.

9. Louis XI (1461–1483) obtained treaty rights to recruit troops in Switzerland in 1474.

10. *See* Chapter 3, page 18.

11. Under Valens, Emperor of the East, in A.D. 376.

12. ". . . that nothing is so weak and unstable as a reputation for power which is not based on one's own strength." Tacitus, *Annals* XIII, 19.

13. That is, Cesare Borgia, Hiero of Syracuse, David, and Charles VII of France.

CHAPTER 14

1. *See* Chapter 1, Note 1. Actually the reference should be to Francesco's descendants: Galeazzo Maria, murdered in 1476; Gian Galeazzo, deposed by his uncle Ludovico il Moro; Ludovico il Moro, deposed in 1500 (*see* Chapter 3, Note 1). Maximilian, deposed in 1515, may also be included.

2. Philopoemen (253–183 B.C.), repeatedly elected general of the Achaean League; Plutarch called him "the last of the Greeks."

CHAPTER 15

1. *See* the concluding paragraph in *The Discourses* Three, XLI.

CHAPTER 16

1. Pope Julius II is said to have made many lavish promises to win election and later sold many ecclesiastical offices in order to fulfill them.

2. The rulers referred to are, of course, Louis XII and Ferdinand the Catholic.

CHAPTER 17

1. At Pistoia in 1501 and 1502 a long smoldering rivalry between two factions, which had been encouraged by the Florentines in order to gain control of the city, broke out into rioting. The Florentine government then sent Machiavelli to settle the difficulties. At first, efforts were made to pacify the leaders of the opposing factions. When these failed, the leaders were banished from the city, but only after much bloodshed. Machiavelli had favored banishing them or executing them at the very outset.

2. "Sore need and my new reign compel these/Deeds, to guard my borders on all sides." *Aeneid* I, 563–64.

3. For a detailed discussion of the conduct of Hannibal and Scipio, *see The Discourses* Three, XXI.

4. Fabius Maximus: Roman Consul and dictator, called "the Delayer" for his fight-and-run tactics against Hannibal after the Battle of Lake Trasimene (217 B.C.). Later he opposed Scipio's aggressive policy.

CHAPTER 18

1. The ideas expressed in this chapter, perhaps the most repugnant to Machiavelli's detractors, should be compared with those expressed in *The Discourses* One, X.

2. Machiavelli's friend, the historian Guicciardini, wrote that it had become proverbial in Rome to say that Pope Alexander never did what he said he would do, while his son Cesare never said what he did.

3. For a contrasting judgment, *see The Discourses* One, LVIII.

4. The unnamed ruler is Ferdinand the Catholic (1479–1516).

CHAPTER 19

1. For Nabis, *see* Chapter 9, Note 2.

2. In 1445.

3. The Parliament of Paris, founded in the reign of Louis IX (*ca.* 1254), was the high court of justice.

4. These ten emperors ruled in succession from A.D. 161 to 238.

5. Marcus Aurelius (161–180), author of the *Meditations,* was the adopted son of Antoninus Pius, whom he succeeded to the purple. He died while directing the war against the Marcomanni in Pannonia (now Austria).

   Pertinax (193) was selected to replace Commodus by the conspirators who had arranged the latter's murder, and the choice was afterward confirmed by the Senate. He was assassinated three months later by the Praetorians, who feared his reforms.

   Alexander Severus (222–235) succeeded Elagabalus, by whom he had been adopted. For a time the celebrated jurist Ulpian and the historian Dion Cassius were his advisers. Prudent and moderate himself, he was influenced by the less admirable character of his mother, Mamaea. He was slain by a group of mutinous soldiers, who may have been encouraged to the act by his successor, Maximinus.

6. *See* Note 14 below.

7. Septimius Severus (193–211): commander of the army in Pannonia, he was proclaimed emperor by his troops after the death of Pertinax, spent most of his reign in army camps, and died in York, England.

8. Didius Julianus (193), a senator, purchased the empire from the Praetorian guards by outbidding his rival Sulpicianus. He ruled only sixty-six days.

9. Pescennius Niger (d. 194): commander of the Eastern armies, he was, like Septimius Severus, proclaimed emperor by his troops after the death of Pertinax.

10. Clodius Albinus (d. 197): governor of Britain and commander of the Western armies, apparently remained neutral until challenged by Septimius Severus, who defeated and killed him near Lyon.

11. Caracalla (211–217): succeeded to the throne along with his brother Geta, whom he soon after murdered. Gibbon labeled him "the common enemy of mankind."

12. Following Geta's murder, some twenty thousand Romans, believed to be his friends or adherents, were put to death by Caracalla. Later, while visiting Alexandria, he ordered a general massacre of the population.

13. The centurion had been incited to the crime by Macrinus. *See* Note 16 below.

14. Commodus (180–192): the self-styled "Roman Hercules," was given poison by his favorite concubine and then strangled.

15. Maximinus (235–238) never visited Italy during his reign.

16. Elagabalus (218–222): elevated to the purple by the intrigues of his grandmother, who claimed he was the son of Caracalla, and by the army at Emesa in Syria, he succeeded Macrinus (217–218) after the latter's defeat and assassination. For Julianus, *see* Note 8 above.

17. The reference is to the Mamelukes (i.e., white slaves) who formed the sultan's guard and, in that position, acquired the power to select his successor (1250–1517).

CHAPTER 20

1. On Pistoia, *see* Chapter 17, Note 1.

2. A "condition of balance" existed between 1469 and 1492, the period during which Lorenzo de' Medici, its chief architect, was ruler of Florence.

3. *See* Chapter 12, Note 15.

4. *See* Chapter 3, Note 15.

5. Pandolfo Petrucci, one of the craftiest despots of his day, managed the affairs of Siena from 1500 to 1512. Implacable in his opposition to Cesare Borgia, he was believed to be the brains behind the conspiracy at La Magione. *See* Chapter 7, Note 11.

6. Niccolò Vitelli, a condottiere, was driven from Città di Castello by the troops of Pope Sixtus IV in 1474 and re-

turned to it following the pontiff's death in 1482. It was then that he dismantled the fortresses.

7. Guidobaldo da Montefeltro, Duke of Urbino, was driven from his duchy by Cesare Borgia in June, 1502. Restored by the conspirators of La Magione (*see* Chapter 7, Note 11) in October of the same year, he was forced to flee again a month later. Before doing so, he ordered the dismantling of his fortresses. He returned again in 1503 after Borgia's fall from power.

8. Long the rulers of Bologna, the Bentivolgi were expelled by Pope Julius II in 1506. Supported by the French, they returned in 1511 and ordered the destruction of fortifications that had been erected by the Pope.

9. For Francesco Sforza, *see* Chapter 1, Note 1. Reliance on the castle tended to make the Sforzas indifferent to their subjects.

10. The event occurred in 1488. The Countess Caterina Sforza was the niece of Ludovico il Moro of Milan.

CHAPTER 21

1. The two chief steps by which Ferdinand achieved the unification of Spain were: (1) his marriage to Isabella, by which Castile and Aragon became one kingdom (1479); (2) the conquest of Granada, by which the Moors were finally driven from Spain (1492).

2. The Marranos: Moslems and Jews forcibly baptized. They were expelled in 1501–2.

3. Ferdinand occupied the African coast from Oran to Tripoli in 1509; his military involvement in Italy began in 1501, with the publication of the Treaty of Granada (*see* Chapter 3, Note 12); his war on France began in 1512 when he joined the Holy League (*see* Chapter 3, Note 2).

4. Bernabò Visconti, Lord of Milan (1354–1385), was noted for his bizarre actions, his passion for hounds—he kept as many as 5,000 of them—and his cruelty.

5. For the events related here, *see* Chapter 3, Note 5. The quoted passage is from Livy XXXV, 48.

6. *See* Chapter 3, Notes 8 and 15.

7. In the war between France and the Holy League (*see* Chapter 3, Note 2), Florence had remained neutral. As a result, when the Holy League triumphed in 1512, it turned upon Florence, brought about the fall of its republican government (in which Machiavelli had been active) and the restoration of the Medici family.

CHAPTER 22

1. Antonio da Venafro: professor of law at Siena, he later became the highly esteemed minister of Pandolfo Petrucci (*see* Chapter 20, Note 5).

CHAPTER 23

1. Pre' Luca (i.e., Luca the priest) Rinaldi: ambassador of Emperor Maximilian (1493–1519).

CHAPTER 24

1. Frederick of Aragon, expelled from Naples in 1501 through the joint operations of the French and Spanish.

2. In Chapters 13 and 14.

3. Philip V of Macedon (221–179 B.C.). *See* Chapter 3, Note 5.

CHAPTER 25

1. That is, in 1506.

CHAPTER 26

1. *See* Chapter 6, Note 2.

2. Doubtless the allusion is to Cesare Borgia. *See* Chapter 7.

3. *See* Chapter 11, Note 9.

4. ". . . for a necessary war is a just war and arms are holy where there is no hope except in arms." Livy IX, 1.

5. Events mentioned in Exodus 14–17, here associated with the recent triumphs of the Medici family.

6. The Taro, on the banks of which the Battle of Fornovo was fought in 1495. Here the French army broke through the ranks of the Italian troops and made good its escape from the peninsula. Alessandria, Capua: sacked by the French in 1499 and 1501 respectively. Genoa: after the overthrow of its aristocratic government by the common people in 1506, the city was forced to capitulate to the French in the following year. Vailà: *see* Chapter 3, Note 15. Bologna: the papal legate in charge of its defense in 1511 abandoned it to the approaching French forces. Mestre: burned by the Spanish troops of the Holy League in 1513.

7. Battle of Ravenna, April, 1511. The Germans were serving with the French, the Spaniards with the Holy League, which was defeated.

8. Petrarch, "Italia Mia," lines 93–96.

NOTES TO *THE DISCOURSES*

BOOK ONE, 2

1. Lycurgus, the legendary Spartan lawgiver believed to have lived in the ninth or eighth century B.C.

2. In 1502, after a revolt in Arezzo had been suppressed, the Florentine constitution was changed to provide for a *gonfaloniere*, or chief officer, who was to keep his post for life. After the sack of Prato in 1512, the republic was overthrown in all but name and the Medici family returned to power.

3. Solon came to power in 594 B.C. Except for two periods, during which he was exiled, Pisistratus was tyrant of Athens from 560 to 527 B.C., when he died. He was succeeded by his sons, who remained in power until about 510.

4. The date of the first tribunate is uncertain. Both 494 and 471 B.C. have some authority.

BOOK ONE, 3

1. The traditional date is 509 B.C.

BOOK ONE, 4

1. That is, from about 509 to 133 B.C. *See The Prince,* Chapter 9, Note 3.

BOOK ONE, 10

1. Agesilaus was King of Sparta (398–360 B.C.) and one of its most able and patriotic generals. Timoleon (410–337 B.C.) slew his brother to prevent his setting up a tyranny in

Corinth. Later summoned to Sicily, he defeated the Carthaginians and established democracies in the Greek cities of the island. Dion, a friend of Plato, expelled Dionysius the Younger from Syracuse. Nabis, tyrant of Sparta (207–192 B.C.), was famed for his cruelty. Phalaris, tyrant of Agrigentum (570–554 B.C.), was also famed for his cruelty. Dionysius the Elder (405–367 B.C.) and the Younger (367–356 B.C.) were both tyrants of Syracuse.

2. Catiline plotted to overthrow the Roman government by force in 63 B.C. during the consulship of Cicero, who obtained evidence of his designs and denounced him before the Senate. He was slain in battle the following year. Few men have been so frequently or so violently condemned as Catiline.

BOOK ONE, 11

1. *Purgatory*, VII, 121–23.
2. *See The Prince*, Chapter 6, Note 3.

BOOK ONE, 12

1. In 396 B.C.
2. Charlemagne captured Pavia, the capital of the Longobard (or Lombard) kingdom in 773. The League of Cambray defeated the Venetians in 1509 (*see The Prince*, Chapter 3, Note 15). The Holy League drove the French out of Italy in 1512 (*see The Prince*, Chapter 11, Note 1). The chief architect of both leagues was Pope Julius II.

BOOK ONE, 58

1. Manlius Capitolinus saved the Capitol from capture by the Gauls in 390 B.C. Hence his name. Later charged with treason, he was condemned to death by the people and was hurled from the Tarpeian rock.
2. Hieronymus was slain by the people of Syracuse in 215 or 214 B.C. after a reign of little more than a year.

3. The Decemvirs: ten magistrates elected from the Senate in 441 B.C. to codify the Roman laws. Given absolute power, they soon began to act tyrannously and were removed.

4. Clitus saved Alexander's life in the Battle of Granicus (334 B.C.), and was later slain by him in a fit of temper during a banquet. Afterward Alexander bewailed his rashness. Mariamne, the wife of Herod the Great, having been falsely accused of adultery, was put to death in 29 B.C. Herod later repented.

5. Scipio Africanus, the hero of Zama (202 B.C.), was charged with accepting bribes in 185.

6. The well-known *vox populi, vox Dei*.

7. In *The Discourses* One, 53, Machiavelli argues that it is difficult to get the people's consent for a policy which appears to involve loss or cowardice, even though it actually involves neither. As an illustration, he cites the case of Fabius Maximus ("the Delayer") whose policy of avoiding a head-on encounter with Hannibal (after 217) was mistaken for cowardice.

8. *See The Discourses* One, 2, Note 3.

9. In *The Discourses* One, 59, Machiavelli asserts that both republican and princely states are prone to break alliances whenever their own survival would be seriously endangered if they honored them. In cases where their survival would not be seriously endangered, however, republics are more inclined to honor their pledges than are princely states.

BOOK TWO, 2

1. That is, Germany.

2. I.e., the Etruscans.

3. *See The Discourses* One, II, Note 3.

4. Now called *Hieron*.

5. *See The Discourses* One, LVIII, Note 2.

6. Corcyra is now Corfu. The incident referred to occurred in 427 B.C.

7. Papirius Cursor: a general in the Samnite wars which came to an end in 290 B.C.

BOOK THREE, 21

1. In the previous discourse, Machiavelli showed that victories have sometimes been won by acts of kindness rather than by acts of terror or force of arms.

2. He took poison in order to avoid being turned over to the Romans by the King of Bythnia.

3. In *Discourses* Three, 22, Machiavelli compares two Roman generals of equal stature but contrary temperament. Manlius Torquatus was harsh and demanding with his soldiers, while Valerius Corvinus was mild and considerate. He praises the conduct of both men, but points out that since the method used by Torquatus could not win the affection of his soldiers, it was particularly suitable for a general serving a republic. Corvinus' method, on the other hand, was particularly suitable for a prince whose status would demand a soldiery personally loyal to him; such a method, Machiavelli adds, could result in danger to a republic.

BOOK THREE, 41

1. In the previous discourse, Machiavelli told how the Samnites tricked a Roman army into the Caudine Forks (321 B.C.), where it was encircled.

SELECTED BIBLIOGRAPHY

The following books, all in English or English translation, will be helpful to the reader wishing further information on Machiavelli, his age, and his influence:

Barincou, Edmond. *Machiavelli*, trans. Helen R. Lind, Evergreen Profile Book 23. New York: Grove, 1961.

Baron, Hans. *Crisis of the Early Italian Renaissance.* Princeton: Princeton University Press, 1955.

Bondanella, Peter E. *Machiavelli and the Art of Renaissance History.* Detroit: Wayne State University Press, 1973.

Burckhardt, Jacob. *The Civilization of the Italian Renaissance.* Garden City, NY: Doubleday, 1960.

Butterfield, Herbert. *The Statecraft of Machiavelli.* London: Bell, 1940.

Cassirer, Ernst. *The Myth of the State.* New Haven: Yale University Press, 1973.

Chabod, Federico. *Machiavelli and the Renaissance*, trans. David Moore. New York: Harper & Row, 1958.

Fleisher, Martin, ed. *Machiavelli and the Nature of Political Thought.* New York: Atheneum, 1972.

Gilbert, Allen H. *Machiavelli's* Prince *and Its Forerunners.* Durham, NC: Duke University Press, 1938.

Gilbert, Felix. *Machiavelli and Guicciardini: Politics and History in Sixteenth-Century Florence.* Princeton: Princeton University Press, 1965.

Gilmore, Myron P., ed. *Studies on Machiavelli.* Florence: Sansoni, 1972.

Hale, John Rigby. *Machiavelli and Renaissance Italy.* New York: Macmillan, 1960.

Hexter, Jack H. *The Vision of Politics on the Eve of the Reformation: More, Machiavelli, and Seyssel.* New York: Basic Books, 1973.

Jensen, De Lamer, ed. *Machiavelli: Cynic, Patriot or Political Scientist?* Boston: Heath, 1960.

Mattingly, Garrett. *Renaissance Diplomacy.* London: Cape, 1955.

Mazzeo, Joseph Anthony. *Renaissance and Seventeenth-Century Studies.* New York: Columbia University Press, 1964.

Meinecke, Friedrich. *Machiavellism,* trans. Douglas Scott. New Haven: Yale University Press, 1957.

Parel, Anthony, ed. *The Political Calculus: Essays on Machiavelli's Philosophy.* Toronto: University of Toronto Press, 1972.

Pocock, John Greville Agard. *The Machiavellian Moment: Florentine Political Thought and the Atlantic Republican Tradition.* Princeton: Princeton University Press, 1974.

Prezzolini, Giuseppe. *Machiavelli,* trans. Gioconda Savini. New York: Farrar, Straus & Giroux, 1967.

Raab, Felix. *The English Face of Machiavelli, A Changing Interpretation, 1500–1700.* London: Routledge & Kegan Paul, 1964.

Ridolfi, Roberto. *The Life of Niccolò Machiavelli,* trans. Cecil Grayson. Chicago: University of Chicago Press, 1963.

Roeder, Ralph. *The Man of the Renaissance: Four Lawgivers: Savonarola, Machiavelli, Castiglione, Aretino.* New York: Viking, 1933.

Rubinstein, Nicolai. *The Government of Florence Under the Medici 1434–1494.* New York: Oxford University Press, 1960.

Schevill, Ferdinand. *A History of Florence.* New York: Harcourt Brace, 1936.

Strauss, Leo. *Thoughts on Machiavelli.* Seattle: University of Washington Press, 1958.

Villari, Pasquale. *The Life and Times of Niccolò Machiavelli,* trans. Linda Villari, rev. ed. New York: Greenwood Press, 1968.

Wolin, Sheldon S. *The Economy of Violence.* Boston: Little, Brown, 1960.

ASK YOUR BOOKSELLER FOR THESE BANTAM CLASSICS

THE PHANTOM OF THE OPERA, Gaston Leroux, 0-553-21376-8
BABBITT, Sinclair Lewis, 0-553-21486-1
MAIN STREET, Sinclair Lewis, 0-553-21451-9
THE CALL OF THE WILD AND WHITE FANG, Jack London, 0-553-21233-8
THE SEA WOLF, Jack London, 0-553-21225-7
TO BUILD A FIRE AND OTHER STORIES, Jack London, 0-553-21335-0
THE PRINCE, Niccolò Machiavelli, 0-553-21278-8
DEATH IN VENICE AND OTHER STORIES, Thomas Mann, 0-553-21333-4
THE COMMUNIST MANIFESTO, Karl Marx & Friedrich Engels, 0-553-21406-3
OF HUMAN BONDAGE, W. Somerset Maugham, 0-553-21392-X
THE BALLAD OF THE SAD CAFE and OTHER STORIES, Carson McCullers, 0-553-27254-3
THE HEART IS A LONELY HUNTER, Carson McCullers, 0-553-26963-1
THE MEMBER OF THE WEDDING, Carson McCullers, 0-553-25051-5
BILLY BUDD, SAILOR AND OTHER STORIES, Herman Melville, 0-553-21274-5
MOBY-DICK, Herman Melville, 0-553-21311-3
ON LIBERTY AND UTILITARIANISM, John Stuart Mill, 0-553-21414-4
THE ANNOTATED MILTON, John Milton, 0-553-58110-4
THE SCARLET PIMPERNEL, Baroness Emmuska Orczy, 0-553-21402-0
THE DIALOGUES OF PLATO, Plato, 0-553-21371-7
THE TELL-TALE HEART AND OTHER WRITINGS, Edgar Allan Poe, 0-553-21228-1
CYRANO DE BERGERAC, Edmond Rostand, 0-553-21360-1
IVANHOE, Sir Walter Scott, 0-553-21326-1
THE COMPLETE WORKS OF SHAKESPEARE (28 vols.)
PYGMALION and MAJOR BARBARA, George Bernard Shaw, 0-553-21408-X
FRANKENSTEIN, Mary Shelley, 0-553-21247-8
THE JUNGLE, Upton Sinclair, 0-553-21245-1
ONE DAY IN THE LIFE OF IVAN DENISOVICH, Alexander Solzhenitsyn, 0-553-24777-8
THE COMPLETE PLAYS OF SOPHOCLES, Sophocles, 0-553-21354-7
DR. JEKYLL AND MR. HYDE, Robert Louis Stevenson, 0-553-21277-X
KIDNAPPED, Robert Louis Stevenson, 0-553-21260-5
TREASURE ISLAND, Robert Louis Stevenson, 0-553-21249-4
DRACULA, Bram Stoker, 0-553-21271-0
UNCLE TOM'S CABIN, Harriet Beecher Stowe, 0-553-21218-4

FIFTY GREAT AMERICAN SHORT STORIES, 0-553-27294-2
SHORT SHORTS, 0-553-27440-6
GREAT AMERICAN SHORT STORIES, 0-440-33060-2
SHORT STORY MASTERPIECES, 0-440-37864-8
THE VOICE THAT IS GREAT WITHIN US, 0-553-26263-7
THE BLACK POETS, 0-553-27563-1
THREE CENTURIES OF AMERICAN POETRY, (Trade) 0-553-37518-0,
  (Hardcover) 0-553-10250-8